Tie a Fly, Catch a Trout

Sam Slaymaker squints to conjure up a trout's view
of a Black Nose Dace in the current. The author always
ties flies at a card table in his living room—and
only when there's snow on the ground.

Tie a Fly, Catch a Trout

S. R. SLAYMAKER II

With fly-tying instructions and drawings by

GEORGE HARVEY

Foreword by Charles K. Fox

HARPER & ROW, PUBLISHERS
New York   Hagerstown   San Francisco   London

To Sally

TIE A FLY, CATCH A TROUT. Copyright © 1976 by S. R. Slaymaker II. All rights
reserved. Printed in the United States of America. No part of this book may
be used or reproduced in any manner whatsoever without written permission
except in the case of brief quotations embodied in critical articles and reviews.
For information address Harper & Row, Publishers, Inc., 10 East 53rd Street,
New York, N.Y. 10022. Published simultaneously in Canada by Fitzhenry &
Whiteside Limited, Toronto.

FIRST EDITION

Designed by Patricia Dunbar

Library of Congress Cataloging in Publication Data

Slaymaker, S R
  Tie a fly, catch a trout.

  Includes index.
  1. Fly tying. 2. Trout fishing. I. Title.
SH451.S6 1976   688.7'9   76–9201
ISBN 0–06–013983–8

76 77 78 79 80 10 9 8 7 6 5 4 3 2 1

CONTENTS

A section of photographs follows page 110

ACKNOWLEDGMENTS

For their kind permission to excerpt portions of my articles from their publications, I extend sincere thanks to the following editors: Lamar Underwood of *Sports Afield;* Jack Samson of *Field & Stream;* Steve Raymond of *The Flyfisher;* Thomas Capstick, Jr. of the Anglers' Club *Bulletin* (the Anglers' Club of New York); G. Dick Finlay of *Fly Fisherman;* Keith Gardner of *Fishing World;* and Sheldon L. Factor of *Trout Fisherman's Digest.* Quotations and partial quotations appear in the following chapters:

In Chapter 1 I have quoted from "Cannibal Bait" in the 1961 *Sports Afield Fishing Annual* and from "New This Season—Natural Streamers," in the March 1962 *Sports Afield.* From *Sports Afield Fishing Annual 1966* I excerpted, for Chapter 3, from "Triple Threat Trout Fly," and from "Summer Strategy for Trophy Trout" in the June 1970 issue of *Sports Afield.*

In Chapter 2 I have used portions of my article "Deadly Any Time, Anywhere," from the June 1971 issue of *Field & Stream.*

From *The Flyfisher,* excerpts were taken from "A Farewell to My Preceptor," #2, 1974, for Chapter 2, and from "Alaskan Grayling Float" in #3, 1974, for Chapter 5.

From the Anglers' Club *Bulletin,* volume 54, 1, Winter 1975,

I have quoted in its entirety my article "A Last Day" for Chapter 3.

The Epilogue, "The Odyssey of a Fly Angling Johnny Appleseed," is largely taken from my article of the same name in *Fly Fisherman* of October 1970.

In Chapter 5 I have used portions of "How to Build a Trout Stream," *Fishing World* January/February 1970.

Parts of "The Fly Angler's Ultimate Challenge," in *Trout Fisherman's Digest* (DBI Books, Inc., edited by David Richey) have been quoted in Chapter 4.

Many thanks to Joseph D. Bates, Jr., for permitting me to excerpt in Chapter 1 portions of the Mickey Finn–John Alden Knight story from his excellent book, *Streamer Fly Tying & Fishing* (The Stackpole Company). I appreciate permission to quote from the late Arnold Gingrich's classic *Joys of Trout* (Crown Publishers, Inc.) in Chapter 2 and Ernest G. Schwiebert's favor for use of his description in Chapter 4 of the Marinaro terrestrial discovery from his fine anthology, *Remembrances of Rivers Past* (The Macmillan Company).

I am very grateful to George Harvey for his splendid contribution, the fly-tying lessons, and to Charles K. Fox for his Foreword and copyreading. Leonard Wright also provided a great service in reading galleys and contributing helpful comments.

Much appreciated, also, is the help and guidance of my editor at Harper & Row, M. S. Wyeth, Jr., and of the very able Sallie Gouverneur and Lynne McNabb, who assisted him.

As always my highest praise is reserved for my hardworking typist, my wife, Sally.

S.R.S.

FOREWORD

THE UNWINDING YEARS have wrought major changes in our game of fly fishing in America for trout and bass, changes both witnessed and accomplished by a single generation of anglers. In order to appreciate the significance of this book it is necessary to sketch briefly the story of fly angling's evolution in this country, emphasizing advances made since the end of World War I.

Prior to World War I delivery of the fly was accomplished with a willowy rod and a light, level enameled line supported by an array of flopping ring rod guides. There was no such thing as shooting the line, nor were there casts over 50 feet. The level leader was 6 feet long, with two dropper loops and an end loop; a wet fly on a short, heavy snell was attached to each. Terminal tackle was made of drawn Spanish silkworm gut that had to be soaked before it could be tied.

Flies were wet, mainly garish attractors, for there were no dry flies, nymphs, or streamer flies. Fly tying was a secretive art, passed on by professionals to their sons or apprentices.

Our forerunners in the East cast to a native population of fish: the Eastern brook trout, often called "speckled trout," the most beautiful fish ever to fan fins in sweet water. Out west, where fishing pressure was minimal, the main natural population was composed of rainbow trout.

The post-World War I era saw a new breed of anglers. They were more inquisitive and more ingenious; many rebelled at the time-honored dicta of their forerunners. They recognized that fly fishing is an art that can be advanced through a knowledge of the sciences of biology, entomology, and chemistry. They wanted to discover *reasons* and would not charge anything to accident. Perception became their proxy for practice.

Brown trout from Germany and Scotland slowly but surely won the hearts of American flycasters. Here was a smart, shy, moody fish that surface-fed well, grew fast and large, and could thrive in water that was not quite cool enough to sustain brook trout. The practice of stalking brown trout with dry flies waxed popular in America. Rod builders put backbone into their sticks, and "snake" guides replaced loose rings. Manufacturers produced heavy tapered lines, which made it possible to shoot line for distance casting and lighter delivery. It also encouraged high back casts, which made practical and pleasant high and effortless false casting, a requisite of dry fly fishing.

Then there occurred an accident in the form of a laboratory spill. The result was nylon, a material that lent itself to leaders and line improvement, not to mention tippets of a finer diameter than anything heretofore tested. And nylon did not have to be soaked before tying.

As a result of these refinements in equipment, a new angling concept took form. There were occasions when anglers found it more rewarding to deceive trout with imitations of natural insects rather than with flies unlike anything in nature. This was the start of hatch matching in America. Thanks to the research of the new breed, nymphs and the feathered and hair minnows became increasingly popular. A do-it-yourself fly-tying cult resulted.

Fly tying was now getting beyond the esoteric stage. And so was fly angling. It dawned on the more purposeful fishermen that both pursuits did not have to be the exclusive province of artists in feathers or the idle rich, an all too common presumption born of the age-old British tendency to consider fly fishing "a gentlemen's sport." Unfortunately, many fly anglers wanted to perpetuate the myth. No doubt it did something for their egos. Their natural desire to buy "club water" lent an increasing aura of exclusivity to fly fishing. All the while politicians appeased "worm dunkers" with the "put and take" stocking of open water on a continuing and ever-expanding basis. Proper trout conservation, however, was dependent on more open water regulated for fly fishing only. Obviously, there was a crying need to "sell" fly fishing to growing numbers of bait fishermen. To their everlasting credit, this has been the signal contribution to trout conservation of both George Harvey and Sam Slaymaker.

In the early 1930s George Harvey began teaching fly tying at Penn State University. His courses, offered by a major institution in a great trout state, gave fly fishing for trout real impetus as a sport for people in all walks. There was so little instructional material available that George was very much a self-taught fly tyer. When he became a college instructor he was ready to pass along new styles of ties, new methods, applicable gadgetry, and new patterns. At the time, the Pennsylvania Fish Commission, through its organ, *The Pennsylvania Angler,* published material by George in which he used line drawings rather than photographs, because he felt that drawings were easier for beginners to follow.

Over the decades, prior to his recent retirement to fish, George Harvey taught fly tying and casting to over 35,000 students at State College and city extension schools, at one of which I was a student. Others learned to tie from his illustrated articles. In addition to teaching, he performed on the casting platform, tested tackle for manufacturers, and guided the second most famous angler having the name of Ike. In his study of feeding responsibilities of trout, a special point of interest of his is the question: Is trout reaction instinctive or is it learned? George Harvey was ahead of his time; his contributions prove that.

Unquestionably George popularized fly tying and fly fishing "to the masses" on a scale heretofore unrealized. In different ways Sam Slaymaker has been a tireless worker toward the same end.

In years, George Harvey is older than Sam Slaymaker; and in miles, the former lives closer to the trout than the latter. The twin interests of fly fishing and the sharing of their experiences with others have brought about the crossing of their paths, and the cause of fly fishing has been well served as a result.

Sam Slaymaker's roots are deep in the rich-land "east end" of Lancaster County, Pennsylvania, where he lives in the historic Slaymaker mansion, "White Chimneys." Several generations of our family have been friends. I have known Sam since he was a boy, when he periodically visited my youngest brother, and I'm proud to claim responsibility for Sam's introduction to fly casting on the Yellow Breeches when he was twelve.

After the completion of twenty–one missions over Germany as a radio operator-gunner in World War II, he entered one of ιhe Cambridge colleges in England, where he majored in history. A deep interest in creative writing resulted.

When he returned from England in 1947 he turned to fly fishing for trout with a demoniac intensity. Stream problems were so fascinating that they became serious challenges, and they stimulated him to share them with others. So the fly-fishing hobbyist sought out his old Lawrenceville English teacher, now a highly regarded outdoor writer and gun expert, one Warren "Lefty" Page, for advice on how to launch an outdoor writing career. The first article submitted to a major publication was accepted; so was the second and the third. Then there followed an assignment. In due course there were many more articles and a book, *Simplified Fly Fishing*.

In a sense the book was the logical culmination of Sam's

previous writings. Through most ran the theme of simplification of the art so that potential converts to flies would not be frightened away. In an article praising the farsighted work of West Virginia cold-water fishery men, Sam coined the term "natural angling" to describe angling for fish in their natural habitat with lures that promote optimum action with minimum harm to the fish.

Sam Slaymaker was the first man in this country—which, no doubt, means in the world—to recognize and to write and talk about the great potential of fly fishing as a conservation measure and a stream management tool. The sad fact is that the vital organs of a fish are high in the throat, and frequently when bait is used the hook is swallowed and the fish dies; whereas fish taken on the fly are lip-hooked and can be returned unharmed. Therefore, the more fly fishing and the less bait fishing, the more caught fish can be returned. The Canadians learned this about their salmon fishing decades ago. *Simplified Fly Fishing*, then, was written for the non-fly fisherman in the hope of making him a convert. A book of this sort was greatly needed. It has, I feel, deservedly become an angling best seller.

Sam did run into conservation roadblocks in unexpected places, officialdom being dominated by hatchery men and the chairmen of the stocking committees of town fish and game clubs. But for his contribution to the advancement of trout conservation, Sam, like George Harvey, received the "Order of the Hat" from the Fly Fishers Club of Harrisburg. He does not consider himself to be a professional fly tyer, but the knowledge of his craft was demonstrated when he designed the famous "little trout" series. The Slaymaker contribution to American angling literature and to fly patterns has been significant, but it is the concept and activity of promoting fly fishing as an asset to faltering conservation efforts that will put a star in his crown.

Between them Sam Slaymaker and George Harvey have helped to expand the numbers of fly anglers to the extent that state conservation officials and "sportsmen's clubs" are being forced to consider the merits of promoting natural angling as opposed to the time-worn practice of "put and take" stocking.

I think that *Tie a Fly, Catch a Trout* will further increase the "fly angling lobby." For there is no question but that many sometime, non-tying fly anglers who read this book will begin to "tie their own" and will consequently become more dedicated anglers—and it's the dedicated angler who today carries the fight for proper trout management.

I don't believe there are any books that treat of both fly tying and fly fishing—or, more specifically, books written both to "sell" fly tying *and* instruct in the art. In a very real sense *Tie a Fly, Catch a Trout* is a logical follow-up to *Simplified Fly Fishing*. In the first book the beginner learns the essentials of the pastime. In the second he is motivated to discover what Sam aptly calls "another dimension" to the sport.

It would be difficult to find two more dissimilar collaborators: George, the poor boy from DuBois, Pennsylvania, who hung around a butcher shop to panhandle fly-tying materials, and Sam, an eighth-generation member of Pennsylvania's squirearchy; George, the clinically meticulous, full-time professional tyer who works in a hideaway study built to hold several thousand dollars' worth of fly-tying inventory, and Sam, who ties only when snow is on the ground and then on a card table in his living room with his family—to the strains of classical music on the stereo.

However, the tying proclivities of each makes for this excellent and truly "different" fishing book. Sam's yarns about the tying and fishing of his flies will surely excite the interest of non-tying and even non-fly-fishing readers. Those who want to learn to tie flies have the old master's time-tested, easy-to-follow lessons to teach them.

—Charles K. Fox

PREFACE

The supreme moment for a fly fisherman is when he presents his furred and feathered imitation naturally enough to dupe a wily trout into seizing it. The angler's satisfaction, of course, derives from his ability to imitate nature. His fly alights like its live counterpart, drifts with the current, and gives the fish an impression of a natural fly.

Such angling calls for finesse superior to that involved in bait fishing, for while there are some very skillful bait fishermen, none is required to imitate nature. Rather, they use nature's actual components—worms, minnows, grasshoppers or helgramites. The bait fisherman's quarry is not duped. He's simply fed and then—ain't it all a dirty shame?—hooked.

Since it is infinitely more challenging to catch fish by fooling rather than feeding them, the fly angler's success is certainly more satisfying, for in imitating natural phenomena with artificial flies he becomes something of an artist. If he ties his own flies, he becomes every bit as creative as the person who paints pictures from nature, and, even better, he discovers a new dimension to fly angling.

Most non-tying anglers fish only a few times each season, if that. These casual or "sometime" fishermen usually feel it is not worth the time or effort to pursue this seemingly tedious hobby. But those who attempt fly tying invariably find it easy to learn, therapeutic, and very rewarding—particularly after taking that first fish on their own tie. Wintertime fly tying will cause them to think fishing year round. Anxious to try their latest offerings, they'll spend more time astream than they used to. Consequently, they will become more compleat anglers.

There are many books on fly fishing, fewer on fly tying, and very few treating both subjects—all of which suggests the unfortunate fact that too many fly anglers consider these pastimes to be separate and distinct. In reality, of course, they are complementary. Complementary, I suggest, because you can't enjoy either to the optimum without being a practioner of both. Hence, this book. It has three purposes: First, my prose contribution is meant to alert the uninitiated to the joys of fly tying. Secondly, the book is designed to instruct them in the art. Its third purpose is to help neophyte fly tyers to fish their own flies with confidence.

I believe that I am well qualified to attempt the first job. For in discovering this often missed extra dimension to fly angling, I've had enough exciting experiences to tempt me to title this book "Adventures in Fly Tying." And many rewarding experiences resulted, too—sometimes through happenstance rather than expertise, since, truth to tell, I am not all that great a tyer. So I toyed with "Confessions of a Fly Tyer." Since I'm not qualified to cope with the instructing part of the book, I was overjoyed when one of the nation's most experienced and respected fly-tying instructors agreed to take on the job.

George Harvey, associate professor and head of required physical education for men at Penn State University for thirty-seven and a half years until he retired in 1973, has here furnished fly-tying lessons that will enable the totally unitiated to tie the first fly in a matter of minutes.

At Penn State George was responsible for teaching more individual fly tyers than anyone else on record. Specifically, he instructed over 35,000 youngsters and adults in angling, casting, and fly tying. In 1943 he organized and taught the first angling and fly-tying classes (non-credit) in the United States (at Penn State). The first accredited university-level angling course in the country was given there by George in 1947. In 1964 he revised in manual form fly-tying lessons disseminated the country over. A longtime contributor to fishing publications, George has advised various tackle companies continuously, instructed in leading fly-fishing schools, conducted 42 angling clinics, and taught many extension classes. A recipient of the coveted "Order of the Hat" from the Harrisburg Fly Fishers Club, George Harvey was also a fishing companion of President Eisenhower, for whom he tied flies.

Fledgling tyers can gain confidence in their own first flies by a stratagem that resulted from a letter I recently received from a fly-fishing minister in the West. He put to me the age-old query: "If you had to pick only five flies to take into a wilderness area for a survival course, which patterns would you choose?" Votes have been taken on this subject for lo these many years. Naturally, the chosen patterns vary widely. But more often than not, respondents tend to pick well-known old favorites—for one very good reason. They know that over the long pull these patterns have been good producers for themselves and others, sometimes for no clearly definable reasons.

Beginning tyers often have misgivings about the effectiveness of their first flies. They can gain confidence by starting with proven prototypes. For example, if you're convinced that the Black Nose Dace is a killing streamer pattern, that's the one to tie first off. For while your tie might not be the last word in artistry, you can be certain that it imitates a successful pattern. The chances of success with your own rendition are increased. Once that first trout is taken on your Dace, you're over a big hurdle—the realization that you can tie a catching fly!

By way of helping neophyte fly tyers develop that all-important confidence factor, George Harvey and I have singled out five patterns in each of the five categories of artificial flies treated in the book—namely, streamers, nymphs, wet flies, dry flies, and terrestrials. A half a dozen leading angler-authors back up our contention that these 25 flies are very effective trout-takers under most conditions from coast to coast. Our dressings for the flies are given after each category's tying lesson.

Perhaps some readers will wonder why none of my own patterns are included, particularly since I describe with such relish their evolution and use (not to mention that some have proven very effective). Quite frankly, I've eschewed their inclusion for a reason other than what the English call "good form." Plainly, their track record is not as good as our chosen patterns for the simple reason that they are of more recent vintage. But in the hope that beginning tyers will try their hands on my offerings (after they've worked successfully on the old stand-bys) I have included the dressings in the chapters, along with others that have proven especially successful.

I am more than grateful to my old friend Charles K. Fox for proofreading, many valued suggestions, and his Foreword. With the assistance of the likes of Charlie—truly a fly-angling author of world renown—and George Harvey, there no longer remained any question about the book's title. For enough valid yet easy-to-understand fly-tying know-how became available to convince me that even beginning tyers who claim to be "all thumbs" can now learn to tie a fly.

Since this book is written principally for those who already know something about fly fishing, its emphasis is not on "how to" fishing methods. Rather, these yarns are meant to be relaxed with. If my sometimes zany, often exciting and always rewarding adventures in tying and fishing inspire non-tying fly anglers (as well as the uninitiated) to turn to George Harvey's lessons with serious intent and thus discover two dimensional fly angling—the better for them to become more "compleat anglers"—I shall count this book a worthwhile effort.

A. R. Haymaker II

1. "The Fly Angler's Crutch for Hatchless Days"

—THE LATE ARNOLD GINGRICH'S
DEFINITION OF THE STREAMER

I TIED MY FIRST TROUT FLY in the winter of 1948. It was a Squirrel Tail streamer (more particularly, a bucktail). My mentor, hovering anxiously to the left flank rear—and then to the right and back again—assured me that this would be a "killing lure." John Stauffer was only trying to be nice, I thought to myself, on that snow-filled December night over 27 years ago, for the dressing sat slightly off center, and the head was deformed and a bit too large. But deep down I sensed that singular form of satisfaction that goes with all the "firsts" of a lifetime.

Soul satisfying, too, was the fly's baptism.

Over watermelon-sized rocks the narrow Pocono mountain stream coursed white into a pool shaped like a horseshoe. Its far extremity glistened dark amber beneath an overhung swatch of flowering rhododendron. Even to my untutored eye the deep cut at the bank was fishy-looking. Perhaps a sense of awe, born of this small glen's matchless beauty rather than fear of spooking fish, was responsible for my stealthy approach. Anyway, after a long, fishless afternoon of sloppy fly presentation, I finally did something right. For as my Squirrel Tail washed from the riffles into the pool, a shadowy, olive-pink

1

blur blotted its shimmering silver tinsel from view. There was no take, just an inquisitive look-see. But it put my heart in close proximity to my Adam's apple.

A whispered suggestion that I rest the fish came from behind.

Startled, I turned to find John Stauffer, now my on-stream mentor, intently watchful. A two-minute wait was all that I could bear. Carefully, I flipped the streamer to the riffles, a few feet ahead. This time it drifted hard by the bank into the deepest water. Just before it disappeared, that varicolored streak flashed again. This time we connected.

As my fish quickly atomized the surface to white spray, John urged me to pay out line. I never had to—the hefty brook trout took it from my fumbling hands. But curving upstream rapids discouraged a protracted run and saved my day. The brookie turned back to the pool. There I fought him simply by hanging on until a series of deep dives and surface splashings wore him out. Thanks to John's asides, I moved into the stretch at the propitious time and netted him. The fish was a 13 1/2-inch deep-bellied native, weighing three quarters of a pound.

This landmark experience inspired me to devour books and articles on fly tying. Most of my first ties were old stand-by imitations of bait fish such as Black Nose Dace, Silver Darter and Gray Ghost. These deceiver patterns seemed more effective for me than the more brightly dressed attractors, particularly when I was fishing over finicky hold-over or stream-bred fish, especially the always more choosy brown trout.

My wife Sally's late uncle, Dr. James P. Trotter, told a story back in 1957 that convinced me that the optimum in streamer effectiveness would be an imitation of a young trout. Here is what happened.

On a spring day in 1897, 16-year-old Jimmy Trotter shadowed an exquisitely outfitted older man for a mile and a half through the woods to a large pool on New York State's Neversink River. An ancient hotel nearby had been Jimmy's headquarters for a couple of years past during early season week-ends. The old gentleman was often there too—forever keeping his distance from the other fishermen, who talked of him in awed whispers, for here was a man who had let it be known that he fished dry flies only. And he always came in with trout —mostly big ones.

But Jimmy had never seen them being caught because the gentleman fished alone. He said that he didn't want to be "disturbed." So Jimmy followed him, knowing that if he were caught, the old hostelry would be forever out of bounds for him. After all, gentlemen anglers of the late nineteenth century just didn't spy on one another!

From behind the tree Jimmy Trotter watched the "expert," who, after furtively glancing upstream and down, laid his rod on the bank. Then he moved into the mouth of a little feeder stream, leaned over, and laboriously lifted a large rock. Hold-ing the rock at chest height, he studied the shallows. Seconds later he hurled the heavy stone down onto the boulders at his feet. The rock-heaving bit was carried on for a full five min-utes. Just when Jimmy was sure that the man was going ber-serk, he saw him reach down and scoop up a small fish. It was obviously a young trout; the feeder streams were full of them.

This "expert" was after live bait, and he was lowdown enough to stun trout fry in order to get it! Sure enough, the spoiler baited up and cast to the riffles at the head of the stretch. The line bellied as the current began to wash the hapless little trout back onto the pool. Then it straightened out, became taut, and started to move forward. A brookie that Jimmy thought just had to go two pounds thumped up to the surface in a gurgling splatter of white water. Jimmy watched two more trout get done in, and then, feeling extreme nausea coming on, he traipsed back to the hotel.

His loathing for the old faker so colored his recollection of the experience that it took Dr. Trotter a long time before he saw the event for what it really was: a basic lesson to be learned by all trout fishermen who would catch more and larger fish, under any conditions, on an artificial lure.

What kind of an artificial can be used at all times and anywhere, whether flies are hatching or not? The streamer or bucktail, of course, the development of which in the 1930s represented a major breakthrough in trout fishing.

Like many fly fishermen during this period, Dr. Trotter was so steeped in the belief that trout and wet flies went together like bacon and eggs that he overlooked the tremendous fish-catching potential of streamers. So he and his partners were skunked sometimes when they could have been bailed out by what they derisively called "Christmas trees." True, early streamers were very largely designed to be things of beauty. While they were meant to imitate small fish, little thought was given by some of their designers as to what kind of fish they ought to look like.

The fact that a streamer can become a real killer when it imitates a specific form of food fish dawned on Doc Trotter in the early 1940s when he was fishing for smallmouth bass in an upstate New York millpond.

He had terrific results with a Mickey Finn type of streamer after the natives had told him "that's all they'll take." Other streamers just hadn't worked for him. One of the natives had a very sensible explanation: The bright yellows and orange-reds of the Mickey Finn make it look like the little pumpkin-seed sunfish that the bass fed on constantly.

Remembering that long-gone day on the Neversink and how viciously the "expert's" big trout went after the little one used for bait, Dr. Jimmy thought to himself that the most effective possible lure for trout ought to be a streamer designed to *look* like a young trout. Trout can be cannibalistic, and any real trout stream provides one constant form of food fish—young trout!

For years the doctor talked to his fly-tying friends about his

4

idea, but nothing came of it until 1957, when the doctor talked me into trying my hand at imitating a young trout with "fuzz and feathers."

Intrigued by the idea of hitting on a good approximation of a brown trout's coloration (I felt a brown would be easier to come by than a brookie), I came up with what seemed a brilliant idea.

An aquaintance employed in a Pennsylvania watch company who developed acetate displays suggested that we place a small trout in a prism, the better to separate the colors for imitation. He cast a two-piece, partially hollowed contraption, and we repaired to a pay-to-fish trout hatchery. The ensuing tableau was something reminiscent of an Abbott and Costello routine. My friend positioned a wiggling four- to five-inch brown trout in his Rube Goldberg prism. It was then held high to the sun while yours truly squinted anxiously to get color readings—which were then ticked off by ballpoint on a paint company's color chart! (I cringe in admitting all of this. But I was young and very much the neophyte with respect to trout lore.)

For months I pondered possible ties for a brown-trout imitation. What would be the most effective body material? Should it be of bucktail or feathered? Since bucktail seemed easier to dye and tie than feathers, I decided on bucktail. A few days after I completed dying, southeastern Pennsylvania was inundated by one of the heaviest snowfalls on record.

That evening in March 1958 the driving blizzard was fast turning into one of the worst climatic catastrophes in the memories of area natives. Devoid of its customary roar from trucks and the whine of tires, the now deserted highway made my farmhouse seem lifeless. The snow's glistening white shroud had embraced lightly at first. Now it was growing heavier by the minute.

Alone—without lights, central heat, phone, or running water—I listened to the periodic roar of crashing pine trees. They

5

were going more rapidly than earlier. Those far out in the grove went with dull thuds; the nearer ones cracked sharply.

The sounds reminded me of antiaircraft fire during the war —all the more so when I realized that waiting for the barn and outbuilding to collapse was very much like anticipating the shell with my number on it. But what had our B-17 crew done about the flak? Nothing. We just sat and took it.

Just the answer, I thought to myself. I would relax and forget about the snow on farm-building roofs. And to stay relaxed I could heed the head shrinkers and turn to something absorbingly constructive like bead stringing. There were no beads, but there was the fly-tying kit.

I was therapeutically productive until far into the snow-filled night, comfortable and warm at a card table by the hearth's blaze, sparkingly animated by tinder-dry pine logs. Four candles and a gasoline lantern provided light that seemed exotically adequate at the time. But the next day's ocular hang-over was to prove conclusively that one should never tie trout flies by candlelight!

Bacon, eggs, and the coffeepot—simmering with snow wa-ter—gave off their familiar smell. It blended with the aroma of burning logs into the singular scents of our Pocono "woods-men breakfasts." Only frying trout were lacking. It was time to dream a bit.

My dream eventually began to focus. I heard the throwing around of waders, the reeling of line, the talk of my compan-ions. Their familiar voices chatted on in this dream world, the essence of which was so strangely mixed up in space and time that I wondered later whether the scene had been experienced before or was yet to be.

The subject was streamers. All agreed that, bucktail-wise, there was one always effective pattern: Art Flick's Black Nose Dace. His imitation proved a killer because it looks to trout like a very familiar food fish. The discussion had turned logi-cally from minnows to trout cannibalism, the habit of eating

6

their own kind. At this point the coffeepot hit a high boil, and I woke up.

My living room and its fireplace were still there. The fly vise and dyed bucktails were ready. I settled down to tying that brown-trout streamer.

Now this took no mean quantity of presumption. For the late, great artist Jack Atherton once told a friend of mine that to his mind no painter had ever truly represented a live trout's hues with paint and brush. Not being an Atherton, small chance that I could hit an adequate color combination with a fly vise by candlelight, let alone with paint and brush. But one of the nice things about fly tying, besides its keeping you off the streets, is that there are no rule books. Pragmatism can reign supreme. You can even tie imitation breadcrumbs, and you'll be judged only on how well they work.

A brown trout's hues, it seemed, should be (from back to belly) dark brown, blending into a lighter brown interspersed very slightly with yellows and reds. The underside, I thought, should be white but ever so slightly tinged with orange-pinks.

Here was the result: Body—white spun wool, intermingled very sparingly with wool dyed orange-pink and wrapped with thin copper wire ribbing that served to highlight the yellow effect, promoting also the quality of iridescence common to fish under water. The top layer of hair was dark-brown squirrel, receding into the next layer, comprising lighter brown squirrel mixed sparsely with strands of dyed yellow and red bucktail. The head: jungle cock. The tail: I removed the dark center of the breast feather of a ring-neck pheasant. Thus, I had a mixture of reds, yellows, and browns around whitish orange-pinks to carry out the basic coloration of the brown trout. I tied up a dozen such streamers while the blizzard raged. They were all dressed on No. 6 long-shank streamer hooks.

Throughout the night I had been oblivious to the storm. When I knocked off in the small, dawn-lit hours, I was at ease.

The snow had tapered off. The buildings had weathered the storm.

On the opening of the 1958 trout season I distributed some brown-trout streamers among friends. Their results matched my own; the new bucktail was as effective as the best of the old stand-by patterns. It produced a startling take for John Stauffer: a monster brown from Spring Creek in Centre County, Pennsylvania. In conversation he referred to it as "the little brown trout." The name stuck.

Many successful experiences with the "Little Brown Trout" led to my doing a piece on it, including tying instructions, in the 1960 issue of *Sports Afield's Fishing Annual*. Within weeks after the opening of the 1960 trout season, I was receiving letters from the country over. Comments were definitely favorable. By midseason it was being manufactured and promoted by the Weber Tackle Company. Other commercial tyers soon picked it up. Over the next four years it was mentioned in at least five magazine articles—maybe more. My mail increased steadily. Some letters were from such famous members of the angler-writer fraternity as Arnold Gingrich, Ernie Schwiebert, and the late John Alden Knight.

Christened by the experts, the Little Brown Trout's future as a streamer pattern was secure.

When writing about the Little Brown Trout I described it as a "natural" streamer, since it was meant to simulate a small trout as opposed to attractor streamers which don't resemble any specific fry fish. The old attractors now left me cold. I stuck almost exclusively to the brownie streamer and such other natural patterns as the Black Nose Dace, Muddler Minnow (a stone catfish or sculpin imitation). Success with these natural streamers inspired me to try for imitations of brook and rainbow trout fry. To professional fly tyer Jack Wise III should go the kudos for helping me design what our confreres considered effective imitations.

8

Here is the tie for the Little Rainbow Trout. Top: strands of barred badger hair, a layer of green dyed bucktail blended into some pink-dyed and some white, all tied sparse. Body: pinkish-white fur with silver ribbing. Tail: green bucktail. Throat: pink bucktail. Eyes: jungle cock.

The Little Brook Trout also has a back of barred badger hair followed by green bucktail and then some orange, blending into white—another sparse tie throughout. Body: cream fur with silver ribbing. Tail: green bucktail from a red tag. Throat: orange bucktail. Eye: jungle cock.

During the 1960 and 1961 seasons both streamers gave good accounts of themselves in Pennsylvania and New York. The brookie streamer proved helpful on those back-country runs containing native brook trout. It gave me one memorable experience in July 1961 when I was the guest of the late Ellis Newman in the heart of the Catskills at Turnwood, New York.

Knowing that I dearly love small native streams, Ellis agreed to put me on one so far off the beaten track that it took a long haul by Jeep over logging roads and deer trails, topped off by a few miles of hiking, to reach it. The rough trek was worth it; the small stream was a jewel. Countless boulders broke its fast-flowing riffles into a long series of little crystal-clear pools.

A caddis fly hatch was on the water. At first matching it and taking one little native after another was fun. But when even the largest of dry flies failed to raise a fish over five or six inches, the time was ripe for a change of pace.

I tied on a Little Brook Trout bucktail and began fishing straight downstream—not in quartering casts, as there wasn't room for orthodox streamer presentation. I simply flicked my No. 10 bucktail into the riffles, let it sink and wash into one of the little pools. Then I'd jerk it back quickly toward the white water at the pool's mouth, giving it the appearance of a baby brookie seeking the protection of fast water.

9

Action began at once—fast and furious. In almost every little eddying stretch, fat crimson natives slashed and thumped at the streamer. With this barefoot-boy technique, I must have picked up and released 25 of those trout that afternoon. Most of them ran between eight and ten inches—by and large the biggest trout in the little stream.

The explanation was simple. My streamer was too big for those small trout that had been monopolizing the dry flies Ellis and I had been using, but it was a good mouthful for the larger, more cannibalistic fish. What with all the native fry in the stream, the Little Brook Trout seemed as natural-looking a lure as you could find.

Almost two decades' worth of water has coursed down my favorite streams since the birth of the Little Brown Trout. Recalling this experience many years later, I'm as embarrassed over the rationale behind the streamer's inception as I am over those gestational antics at the hatchery. In the first place, I should have realized that trout fry the size of a streamer can't sport adult colors. Secondly, with all due respects to Dr. Jimmy Trotter's convictions about trout cannibalism, I'm now persuaded that the best all-around criteria for bait-fish imitations is simply a fishy appearance. In sun-dappled shallows the sides and bellies of small fish emit sporadic flashes, so a streamer body with sufficient tinsel to create a flash is a great plus. But like most minnows, the top side should have rather dull coloration.

Were it possible to divine the truth about the effectiveness of the Black Nose Dace, it's pretty safe to surmise that the "flash" provided by its fully tinseled body and white flank, contrasted with the dark bucktail back, is more deadly than that hallmark black streak. This is not to suggest that impressionism is not an important factor. In stream currents trout can get only a fleeting view of their quarry—rarely a long look. This is fortunate, for trout then see a rough approximation of the size and hues of fish fry food. This is what I really "developed" with the Little Brown Trout—a rough approximation of *any* small fish. The subdued coloration, I've come to believe, was of more moment than the color scheme. But of course one can never be positive about this theory in all situations.

Last summer in the Poconos, while fishing a Little Brook Trout streamer, I caught a 15-inch, deep-girthed, hold-over or stream-bred brownie. When the hook was removed a five-inch native brook trout was disgorged. How pleasing it was to muse about the effectiveness of my brainchild! Maybe that wily brown really *was* conned into taking my Little Brook Trout streamer for a second course!

Over the years, though, the Little Brook and Rainbow streamers were not as successful as the Little Brown, nor, for that matter, a wide range of old stand-by natural *and* attractor patterns. And if I still harbored beliefs about the key to their effectiveness lying in their likeness (colorwise) to brook and rainbow fry, said beliefs were disabused by the famous outdoor writer Erwin Bauer, who in an *Outdoor Life* piece billed these two streamers as excellent lures for crappie! So much for selective cannabalism.

I finally came to the obvious conclusion. The brookie and rainbow streamers perform like the bright, attractor patterns that they are. The Brown Trout streamer, with its more subdued coloration, is a more natural-appearing deceiver. Hence, in the long run it has proven itself the most productive. For all bait-fish imitations attract. But, as noted, duller ones have the advantage of appearing more natural to fish. None is more dull—even ugly—than what is probably, by general agreement, the most killing streamer ever devised: Don Gapin's Muddler Minnow, of which more later.

A reader of this soliloquy on streamer theory might well note that I've come full circle on the subject. In total ignorance I approached it years ago, pseudo-scientifically, only to conclude in the end that no definitive answers were forthcoming.

So why dwell on this matter here? Simply to demonstrate the fact that fly tying heightens the contemplative side of fly angling. Thanks to the creative effort involved, contemplation *can* lead to solid, scientifically oriented discoveries. One is reminded of Halford's evolving of dry fly practice, Skue's development of nymph imitations, the Marinaro–Fox terrestrial insect breakthrough, and, lately, Leonard Wright's caddis fly investigations. Or contemplation can lead to empirical—even slapdash—approaches, such as my own, which resulted in the very effective Little Brown Trout.

While there are bound to be new imitative discoveries in scientific fly development, we can be pretty sure that few will be made by "sometime" fishermen. As always, such work is the province of dedicated, longtime experts. But fly fishing is more an art form than a science. Even beginning duffers can aspire to artistry with rod and line astream and with vice and bobbin at hearthside.

Since my experience in streamer development had its humbling side, I determined to eschew "science" for art. I would endeavor to become an improved tyer as well as a fisher of accepted patterns, and I would drink deeply from the literary wells of my betters.

Among the many streamer patterns that I tied and fished, five old stand-bys were my favorites—the Muddler Minnow, the White Maribu, the Skykomish, the Mickey Finn, and the Black Nose Dace. It is not to denigrate other patterns—old-timers or more recent innovations—when I recommend these five streamers to beginning tyers as superb producers. It could be that I fished them too much at the expense of others simply because of their fame and that others would have scored as well. Still, these patterns *did* produce well so consistently that I judge them great confidence builders for beginning tyers. And I'm backed by some experienced angling friends, such as Charlie Fox, Jim Bashline, Boyd Pfieffer, Don DuBois, and

Lefty Kreh. Interestingly, most of these streamers have distinguishing features which in some measure could be responsible for their effectiveness. For example, the Muddler Minnow is particularly deadly because it can be used as a "triple threat" lure.

John Stauffer used to stress the deadliness of any large dry fly fished after a rain squall. His theory was that wind and rain are bound to shake terrestrial insects of all sizes and types from streamside foliage, the largest affording trout the most fetching mouthfuls. He had proven this point to me occasionally in the Poconos.

After a midafternoon downpour on New York's Neversink, John pawed over my fly box, dug up a Muddler Minnow streamerette (a small streamer) and advised me to "grease it good" and fish it dry by way of simulating a water-stranded cricket or grasshopper. As such it was unbeatable. I don't know how many trout gobbled the thing. All the while three other companions assiduously matching a light Cahill hatch came off definitely second best. So as a quartered subsurface streamer and a dead-drift dry fly the Muddler Minnow is a superb lure. I often fish it "on top" upstream during grasshopper season (late July) in the Poconos with gratifying results.

The Muddler is so ugly-looking that it bears a strong resemblance to various kinds of large nymphs. When it's rolling along the bottom, fish get the effect of a big nymph that has just left its moorings and is getting ready to hatch. The Muddler, then, can be used effectively dry, wet, or as a bait-fish imitation.

On cloudy days and during evening hours a most killing streamer is the White Maribu, because in darkened waters it presents a massive, whitish sheen. After-dark fly-fishing specialist Jim Bashline leans toward dark patterns for night fishing. While other experienced anglers agree, the White Maribu has got, I believe, to be considered an exception to this rule. For I have consistently scored very well with it at night,

13

as have many of my friends. And its supple flank feathers can be made to breathe very well—to pulsate—when it's jerked against the current. After dark larger trout tend to lose some of their inhibitions and to go for the White Maribu with a terrifying vengeance. By far this has always been my favorite after-sunset streamer.

When fishing Western trout waters a "must" streamer is the Skykomish. Perhaps an experienced Western angler can explain why this fly is vastly more productive than so many of the favored old-time Eastern patterns. I found out about the Skykomish the hard way years ago in Alberta when fishing the Spray River. The guide told me to use it, and it produced consistently. For the better part of two days I used my favorite Eastern patterns and did not do too well. But when I switched back to it, strikes picked up noticeably. Again, in 1972, when fishing in Alaska with the well-known guide Mike Hershberger, our party scored heaviest with the Skykomish. I spent most of my time dry-fly fishing for arctic grayling, so my streamer fishing for trophy rainbows was limited. But none of the Eastern patterns that I used scored as well as that premier Western streamer, the Skykomish. I've never used it much in the East, so I'm no judge of its effectiveness there. Anyone who streamer fishes the West should have a good supply with him.

Probably the catchingest of all brook-trout streamers is the late, great John Alden Knight's Mickey Finn. Colorwise there is no good reason for its charm over brookies—particularly wild ones. I suppose that the most reasonable answer is that it's highly visible and, hence, a first-class attractor. The beautiful brookie—the dumb blonde of the trout family, as Arnold Gingrich described it—is a particular patsy for attractor patterns. As noted, the Mickey Finn also spells murder to smallmouth bass.

The streamer that I've used more than any other over all the years is the Black Nose Dace. (I'm not sure why, for the Muddler is by all accounts the best.) I suppose I like the Dace so much because it's the best possible representation of that most common food fish found in trout waters everywhere. Notwithstanding my jaded view of streamers' deceiving power, I still harbor a deep-down hankering to imitate nature—not strong enough, though, to prompt more bait-fish imitations but strong enough to give rise to musings by a firelit hearth about whether or not the Black Nose Dace in my vise will appear as realistic to trout as I think—or hope!—it looks. I squint my eyes and view it hazily, impressionistically, as would a trout through a ruffled bit of pocket water. Sooner or later during these winterset evenings my thoughts turn to trout in a favorite Pocono mountain stream—my "glistening children." I conjure up visions of the fish lying beneath pillows of snow and girded about by frosted films of ice—fragmented, congealed into fearsome forms by gurgling water. The trout are lying stark and sticklike. In a somnolent daze they subsist on their waning supply of fat until spring light dissolves the ice and stirs their primal urge to feed on stirring fly life—and fish fry, for their winter-depleted torsos require some substantial food.

Early spring is streamer time. I relish the thought, moisten the Black Nose Dace's bucktail, adjust the tensor light, squint again. It looks more deceiving! Comes the time to wet it with serious intent in that stretch of stream I've just been mind-picturing, I'll relish memories of the first wetting of the feathers and my impressionistic viewing after the family turns in and the logs have become tangerine-colored embers.

Somehow, recollections of that winter evening at the vise will inspire a more painstaking presentation of the Dace in early season. I'll be more intent during the quartering so as to connect solidly with a lightninglike strike. Indeed, when it comes, I'll be hard put not to believe that I've wished it into happening! Though it may seem far out, I really do believe that there is something to the belief of my old friend, outdoor TV impresario Harry Allaman, that the most successful angler is he who expects each cast to produce! Perhaps such expectations are often borne out because the angler is instinctively more alert. Each success makes him more confident. And the confident angler has more going for him than the fellow who is in doubt about picking the right fly.

The pleasures that inure in fishing your own ties successfully are surpassed by those experienced when others score well with them.

When, in 1966, the Pennsylvania Fish Commission celebrated its centennial I was asked to tie a commemorative fly. I came up with a streamer which the commission named the Golden Palomino. After the Executive Director, Bob Bielo, and I presented the original to Governor Ray Shaeffer, my good friend and professional tyer Ed Shenk produced the flies in great quantities. Individually skin-packed, they were widely disseminated. The tie: Hook: No. 8, long shank. Tail: golden pheasant fibers. Body: ruffled gold tinsel. Wing: red bucktail, badger neck hackle on top. Throat: orange hackle fibers.

A year or two later I was talking on the phone with Warren Page, then *Field & Stream*'s gun editor. Warren said, "Someone here wants to talk to you!" and a chap whose name has since escaped me recounted a tale about the Palomino that is incredible.

While fishing with a group in Labrador (or Newfoundland) he was placed, alone, on a totally deserted stretch of water. After the plane left he discovered that his fly box had been left behind. Then he remembered the Palomino streamer in his wallet. It had been enclosed with a Pennsylvania Fish Commission mailing. In short order he hooked a large squaretail that broke the leader.

A few days later far downriver another member of the party caught the same fish with the Palamino in its mouth! This, in wilderness country with zillions of fish! I got a great kick out of knowing that my concoction was responsible for this "fish story," which bids fair to top the best of them!

And only a short while ago I experienced what has to be the epitome of satisfaction for a fly-tying angler.

I was flying from Winnipeg to Philadelphia after a business trip, lazily splitting glances between the snow-blanketed prarics of Minnesota and the pages of the March 1975 issue of *Field & Stream* magazine. On turning to the results of *F & S*'s 1974 fishing records (the fly section), I noted that one George M. Borso, on the Broadback River in Quebec on September 13, had caught the year's largest brook trout, weighing nine pounds eight ounces on a "Brook Trout streamer!"

My once-in-a-lifetime experience was rendered especially exciting by virtue of the fact that Mr. Borso's big brook trout capture vindicated the cannabalism theory that had prompted me to conceive the streamer. And now, lo and behold, at the time of my above-mentioned revisionist theorizing about trout cannabalism, the damn thing rang the bell in the most celebrated fishing contest of them all!

But what the streamer looked like to Mr. Borso's prize trout isn't important to me. It's enough to revel in the knowledge that the fly succeeded so well that its notoriety will cause more anglers to enjoy using it, successfully, I hope.

The *real* satisfaction resulting from what my friend Jim Bashline calls my "distended vicarious accomplishment" is akin to that felt by a successful landscape artist. Like him, I felt the pleasures of creation and exalted in popular approval (if a valid comparison can be made between a favorable review of a canvas in, say, the National Gallery and a streamer's being listed with the North American record catches of *Field & Stream*!).

Even if these standout happenings hadn't transpired, I still have the matchless pleasure of sharing my ties with other anglers. The vicarious kicks I've always experienced on learning about successes my flies have afforded others are inexplicable. All I can say is that I relish such occurrences more and more as the years unwind.

It might well be argued that a given fly pattern's popularity rests as much (or more) on its notoriety as on its effectiveness as a fish catcher—that a writer can successfully plug any kind of pattern he chooses to dream up. But I submit that this route offers pitfalls enough to the nerviest of promoters. In the first place, unreasonable claims are easily discerned by experienced outdoor editors. Secondly, publicized new patterns are as avidly sought as they are fished by thousands of anglers, so that if one gets poor or even so-so results, discredit will be heaped on its originator. Then, too, there's precious little prior art left in streamer technology. The two most significant developments in recent years are probably the use of mylar and keel hooks. Most bait fish have already been imitated. Of course, who knows what new and successful color combinations might yet be evolved, obtained from further research in piscatorial optics, resulting, perhaps, from such useful studies as Mark Sosin and John Clark's recent book *Through the Fish's Eye* (Harper & Row).

The simple fact is that one's innovative abilities are much more restricted by fur, wool, and fabrics than by wood, metal, and plastics. Thus, we have a plethora of bait-casting Rube Goldberg gimcracks coming on the lure market to appease the tastes of the spin-casting fraternity. Fly innovating generally results from the more honest motives of fly tyers, be they of the sometime living-room variety (like myself), the "wood shedders" (who supply stores and catalogue houses), or the expert fly angler-cum-entomologists, such as George Harvey.

Many innovative fly patterns are developed by non-writers. A tyer-angler will often come up with something that proves a world-beater—word will get around, and sooner rather than later an outdoor writer will contact the innovator, fish the fly extensively enough to satisfy himself that it has merit, and then write about it. This has happened many, many times, a dramatic example being the story of the Mickey Finn.

The late John Alden Knight was given a streamer known as the Red and Yellow bucktail by a friend. After a couple of seasons of successful use Mr. Knight had a fabulous time with it in Canada while fishing for native Square Tails. Gregory Clark, a feature writer from the Toronto *Star*, dubbed it the "Mickey Finn." From Joe Bates Jr.'s classic *Streamer Fly Tying and Fishing* I quote the rest of the story as Mr. Knight wrote it for Joe Bates:

In the fall of 1937 I made an arrangement with *Hunting and Fishing* magazine and with The Weber Tackle Company to write a story about the "Mickey Finn for Hunting and Fishing." The Weber Company took a full-column advertisement in that issue and featured the fly and yours truly in it. The magazine appeared on the news stands when the Sportsmen's Show was on in New York. In the space of two days not a single copy of *Hunting and Fishing* magazine could be found on the New York news stands. I suppose that the name and the flashy colors struck the public fancy. In any event the fly tyers at the show were busy for the entire week tying Mickey Finns. Each night bushel baskets of red and yellow bucktail clippings and silver tinsel were swept up by the cleaning crew at Grand Central Palace, and by Friday of that week not a single bit of red or yellow bucktail could be purchased from any of the New York supply houses. It was estimated that between a quarter and a half million of these flies were dressed and distributed during the course of that show. . . .

During the next few months the entire facilities of the Weber company were stretched to the breaking point in their frantic efforts to keep up with Mickey Finn orders. One outfit in Westchester actually saved itself from bankruptcy proceedings by specializing intensively in the manufacture of Mickey Finns. As matters now stand, it is a difficult thing to find any angler on any stream anywhere who has not at least one Mickey Finn in his kit. The "Mary Pickford" trophy for the prize brook trout taken annually in Ontario was won for the next two consecutive seasons with

Mickey Finn flies. I still use the fly and find it to be a consistent fish-getter.

It should matter not at all to tying anglers if they don't concoct a world-beater fly like the Mickey Finn. Of more moment is the ability to tie flies that catch fish. George Harvey's excellent instructions following will enable the tyro or inexperienced tyer to do this.

These already discussed, longtime, tried-and-true streamer patterns have been chosen: Black Nose Dace, Mickey Finn, Muddler Minnow, White Maribu, and Skykomish. Once a beginning fly tyer takes fish on his own first ties of these well-proven patterns and sufficient confidence is bred in his ability to continue to do so, he then, of course, can work on other well-established streamer patterns such as Keith Fulsher's Thunder Creek series, the Optic group, and many others. And I hope that he will include the Little Trout series.

FLY TYING

Fly tying and fly fishing are complementary. The fly fisherman who learns the skills of fly tying will also be a more proficient angler. The personal enjoyment one derives from this creative and artistic hobby is immeasureable. It not only keeps one occupied with the sport during the off season but also may be a profitable recreation for one's leisure time.

Quality flies today are quite expensive, and the angler who ties his own should be able to take a good many more angling trips just by the money he saves tying his own flies.

Fly tying is a hobby that is easy to master. I have never had one student who could not tie flies well enough to catch fish. This should be convincing enough for the neophyte, because I have taught many thousands this fine art since 1934. I am sure if you follow the techniques described in this book it will not be long before you will be taking fish on your own creations.

Only the essential tools and materials will be listed. As you become more proficient or as your pocketbook allows you will probably want to add additional equipment. There are many reputable companies in the United States and most will send you a catalogue for the asking. Most advertise in sportsmen's magazines.

Tools:

(1) Vise, bobbin, scissors (preferably sharp-pointed), hackle pliers and dubbing needle are the most essential. In addition one could purchase a whip finisher, hackle gauge, scalpel, half-hitching tool, tweezers, and flat-nosed pliers, but these are not really necessary.

Hooks:

(2) Sizes #8, 10, 12, 14, 16, 18, 20, and 22 with regular-length shanks are the most popular for dry and wet flies and nymphs.

Sizes #2, 4, 6, 8, and 10 long shank hooks for bucktail and streamer flies.

Sizes #2 to 3/0 for deer hair bass bugs and flies for larger freshwater fish.

Most freshwater hooks have bronze finish.

Most saltwater flies are tied on cadmium-plated, nickel-plated, tinned or stainless-steel hooks to prevent the corrosive action of salt water. However, I prefer to use freshwater hooks, because if one loses a fish the hook will soon disintegrate and not harm the fish. Hook sizes from #4 to 3/0 are the most popular, because flies tied on larger-size hooks are very difficult to cast.

As you progress you will probably want to purchase hooks for specific flies—i.e., midges, spiders, variants, and nymphs.

Tying thread:

Thread size depends on the hook size and material used to construct a fly.

#2–0 to D for bucktail, streamer and deer hair bass bugs.

#4–0 to 8–0 for smaller flies.

You should always use the smallest-size thread possible for the fly you are tying. This will make for a neater and stronger fly, because many more turns may be taken without building up bulk.

Hackles:

You should have both wet and dry hackle in the following colors: dark brown, ginger, light ginger, cream or straw color, grizzly, black, and blue dun. There are dozens of colors and shades available, but 90 percent of all flies are tied from the colors named.

Body materials:

Chenille, dubbing (underfur from any animal that is fine enough to spin on thread), peacock herl, quill (stripped from primary flight feathers, stripped hackle), silk and synthetic floss, spun fur, and tinsel are the most common. Any other durable material that can be wound on a hook may be used.

22

Wing material:

Wing quills from any bird that have fibers long enough for the size fly you are tying are used for both dry and wet flies. Breast and flank feathers from mallard, wood duck, teal, and hackle tips are used for many patterns. Back and breast feathers are used for cut wings. In addition, hair wings are quite popular. Some of the most common hair used is from deer, squirrel, polar bear, badger, groundhog, and fox. Hair wings are without a doubt the most durable wing material and may be substituted for feather wings if the color is close to the wing material called for in the pattern you are tying.

Tails

Throat and spade hackles are the best for dry flies. Use material listed for wet flies, streamers, and nymphs.

Streamer and bucktail flies:

Saddle hackle, large neck hackle and maribou, natural or dyed, are used for feather wing streamers. Deer-tail hair, natural or dyed, and any other hair that is long enough and the desired color may be used for hair wing or bucktail flies.

Lacquer:

Finish off fly with waterproof lacquer or head cement. Be sure it is fast-drying.

I would like to make it clear that even the best fly tyer cannot produce a quality dry fly with poor material. The fly and workmanship will look excellent, but the fly will not float the way it should; so one should purchase or collect the best-quality dry fly hackle available.

Sizing and selection of hackle for both wet and dry flies is important, and one should be sure that the length of the fibers is the same for every fly tied on the same size hook.

Diagram #1: Shows the important parts of a hook and how to size the hackle. Hackle fibers should be from one and one half to two times as long as the gap of the hook. It is usually necessary to strip and discard the fibers from the lower third of the hackle, so hackle should be gauged by selecting the fibers from the center third.

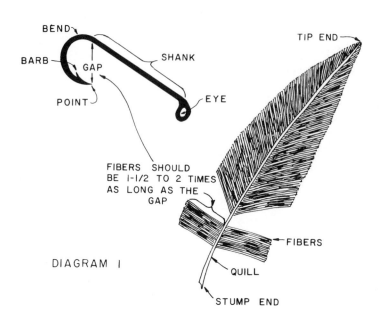

BEND

BARB

GAP

POINT

SHANK

EYE

TIP END

FIBERS SHOULD
BE 1-1/2 TO 2 TIMES
AS LONG AS THE
GAP

FIBERS

QUILL

STUMP END

DIAGRAM 1

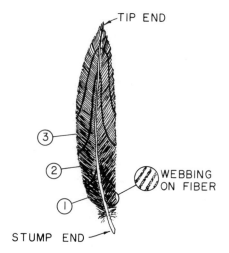

TIP END

③

②

WEBBING
ON FIBER

①

STUMP END

GRADES OF HACKLE

DIAGRAM 2

24

Diagram #2: Shows the various grades of hackle for both wet and dry flies. Any feather from any bird, if the fibers are long enough for the hook size you are tying on, may be used for wet fly hackle. However, 99-plus percent of all dry flies are tied from cock's hackle.

The qualities you look for in a dry fly hackle are: a hackle that is long and narrow from tip to stump end, with short, stiff, glossy fibers that have a minimum amount of webbing and with a mid-rib that is flexible enough to be wound on the hook without twisting. There are all degrees of quality. Only three will be shown in the diagram: #1 is top-quality dry fly hackle, #2 is fair dry fly hackle, #3 is excellent wet fly hackle. The numbers point to amount of webbing; all the rest of hackle is web-free.

Before you start to tie the first fly you should practice how to hold the bobbin, how to attach the tying thread to the hook, and how to throw on a half hitch to finish off the fly. The whip finish will also be diagrammed.

Diagrams #3, 4, and 5 show the above.

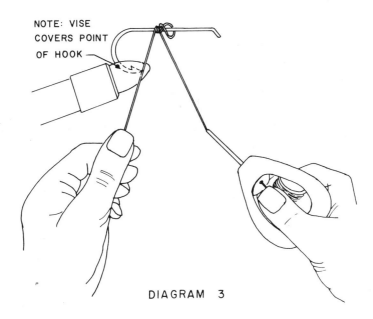

NOTE: VISE
COVERS POINT
OF HOOK

DIAGRAM 3

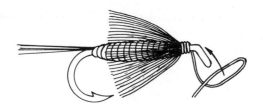

FLY FINISHED WITH
A HALF-HITCH KNOT

DIAGRAM 4

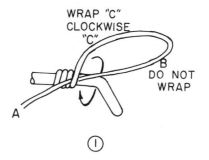

WRAP "C"
CLOCKWISE
"C"
B
DO NOT
WRAP
A

①

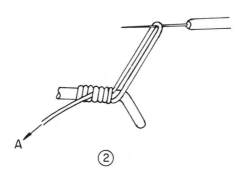

A

②

DIAGRAM 5

SUGGESTED STREAMER PATTERNS

Name	Head	Tail	Ribbing	Body	Tip	Hackle	Wing
Black Nose Dace	black with yellow-black dotted eye	short, red tag: yarn or dyed bucktail		silver tinsel			white, black, brown bucktail
Mickey Finn	black with yellow-black dotted eye			silver tinsel			yellow, red, yellow bucktail
Sky-komish Sunrise	white	yellow and red hackle bar-bules	silver tinsel	claret chenille	silver tinsel	yellow and red	white hair
Muddler Minnow	(cheek) flaired deer hair	mottled turkey		gold tinsel			belly brown or white bucktail; wing mottled turkey quill
White Maribu	white			silver tinsel		(throat) red hackle or red maribou	white mari-bou, pea-cock sword, laid in so it will curl down: three to four strands

Bucktail-streamer fly:

Hair wing, feather wing, and maribou streamer flies are without doubt the most versatile flies for all species of fish. They are especially effective for the fisherman who fishes primarily for large trout.

They are an excellent fly for the beginning fly tyer, because they are easy to tie and are usually tied on larger-size hooks. In addition, most beginners must learn how to hold and wind on material, and on the larger flies this is much easier to do.

When one first starts tying flies one is prone to experiment with various color combinations. Strange as it may seem, it will be impossible to tie a bucktail or streamer fly that will not take fish.

Diagram #1: The first fly illustrated and described will be a bucktail with a tinsel body.

Attach tying thread to hook close to eye as diagrammed. Cut one end of the tinsel to a tapering point and tie this end in at point marked "start." By tapering this end the tinsel will be easier to start and will wind on smoothly. Wind tinsel clockwise up to bend of hook, then back to starting point and tie off as diagrammed.

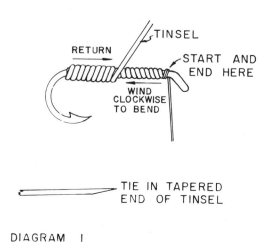

DIAGRAM I

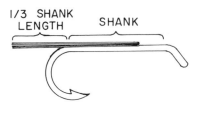

1/3 SHANK LENGTH   SHANK

DIAGRAM 2

Diagram #2: Most bucktails and streamers have no tail, but if one is tying a pattern with a tail, it is best to have tail material that is long enough to extend under the entire body. This will help to keep the body smooth, even, and hump-free. If this is not followed it will be impossible to have a hump-free tinsel body.

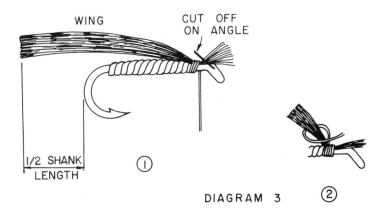

WING   CUT OFF ON ANGLE

1/2 SHANK LENGTH   ①

DIAGRAM 3   ②

Diagram #3 illustrates the method of tying on the hair wing. Cut section of hair near roots, about one and one half times the length of the hook. Hold by root end and pull out all long hairs from the tip end and put back in main bunch so ends are as even as possible.

Most beginners have a tendency to use too much hair. It is better to be a little sparse than too heavy. This is especially true when several colors are used.

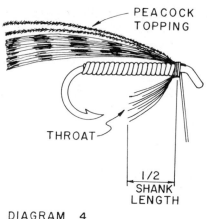

PEACOCK
TOPPING

THROAT

1/2
SHANK
LENGTH

DIAGRAM 4

Before tying in deer-tail hair have tying thread about one fourth back of eye. Now hold hair, as illustrated, on top of hook. Bring tying thread up between thumb and hair, over top and down the other side between index finger and hair. Squeeze tightly and draw up tying thread tight by pulling straight down. Repeat several times, then cut off excess hair at angle, as shown in diagram. If topping or throat is desired, add as illustrated in Diagram #4. If pattern calls for shoulder, it may be added as illustrated in Diagram #5. When preparing shoulder I advise you

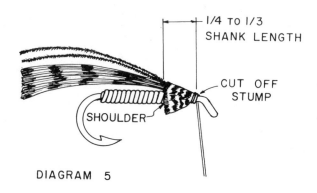

1/4 TO 1/3
SHANK LENGTH

CUT OFF
STUMP

SHOULDER

DIAGRAM 5

strip off fibers until the two feathers are identical in size, but leave the quill long. Tie in by quill, then pull quill until the shoulder feathers lay flat on both sides and are exactly the same length. If you pull just a little of the feather under the tying thread, it will hold it in position and not twist out of line.

Feather-wing streamers are tied using the same sequence. After the body is wrapped, take four matching hackle (saddle or large neck hackle), two on each side, with bottom or concave sides facing each other. Have ends even. Strip off fibers from stump end until you have the desired length, then hold as tight as possible and tie in, using the same procedure as described in the hair wing fly.

Diagram #6 will show the order in which materials are tied on for a combination bucktail and feather-wing streamer such as the popular Gray Ghost.

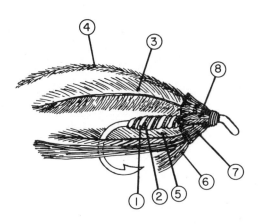

① BODY	⑤ BELLY
② TINSEL OR RIBBING	⑥ THROAT
③ WING	⑦ SHOULDER
④ TOPPING	⑧ EYE

DIAGRAM 6

2. "The Fleeting Brown Wink Under Water"

—FROM G. E. M. SKUE'S DOGGEREL
IN DEFENSE OF THE WET FLY

RECENTLY I HONORED a long-standing invitation of George Harvey's to fish that gem among central Pennsylvania's trout streams, Spruce Creek. Our outing was scheduled to coincide with the early-June emergence of the fabled Green Drake hatch. When we began fishing in midmorning the first large drakes were beginning to flutter from amber-tinted glides. Trout paid little attention to them.

"Too early," George told me. "The feeding orgy will begin later. Best we go with nymphs for a while."

The Green Drake nymph seemed the logical choice. But George suggested one of his large stone fly nymph patterns. Since this nymph had been very effective over recent days he was pretty sure that trout would still be on it; he chose the safe bet lure because he wanted my first trip to Spruce Creek to be memorable. The stone fly nymph was indeed a safe bet—for George. Within 20 minutes he caught nine brown trout, ranging from 11 to 13 inches, while I hooked and lost one heavy brown. Since we used dead-ringer nymphs, I should have done much better. My problem was submerged obstacles. I hooked them while George hooked trout.

Even after taking into consideration all the "givens" of the situation—weighted nymphs, unfamiliar water, my 30 years of experience versus George's 60 (not to mention the fact that I'm not George Harvey)—this miserable performance brooked no excuse save one: On this particular occasion I lacked that indescribable something known as "the nymph fisherman's feel."

Writings on nymph fishing invariably describe the frustrations inherent in the angler's careful watching, during the nymph's drift-back, for the line to stop. Is it a fish or a rock? The strike must be a light one, the books say, just strong enough to set the hook and weak enough to preclude deep imbedding in ubiquitous sunken limbs, patches of moss and weeds. If a rock is fouled, we're told, line should be roll-cast forward, never pulled back hard. Most texts on nymph fishing dwell on the importance of water reading. But no matter how well you divine the presence of subsurface obstacles from tell-tale surface tracery, nymphs can make for tedious, time-consuming fishing—particularly weighted ones, presented on freestone streams. And—excluding "flymphs," of which more later—the most effective nymphs *are* weighted, since it's important that they ride deep, where trout expect to find them. And with most American trout waters being of the freestone variety, it's small wonder that many fly anglers shun nymphs. I've become convinced that some dry fly purists are just that simply because they can't fish nymphs successfully. Rather than admit to the fact, they eschew them, considering them little better than live bait.

Typical of this school was a distinguished Episcopal rector with whom I used to fish in the Poconos. On one occasion I was murdering trout in high water with a weighted Leadwing Coachman nymph, and he did zilch with a dry fanwing Royal Coachman. All day he refused a proffered Leadwing. Late in the afternoon he relented and was very soon snagged. Red-faced with anger, he shouted at me, "Second Samuel [he called my father by the Biblical appellative First Samuel], nymphs are a pain in the ass!"

In those long-gone days I fished nymphs only when conditions allowed nothing else, but eventually I became an inveterate exponent of nymphs and wet flies, fished dead drift. Indeed, I fished dry only when there was surface activity and used streamers and streamerettes principally for fish-finding on unfamiliar water when surface activity was at a minimum. My infatuation with sunken flies developed when it became obvious that, by and large, they are the most efficient of trout decoys.

Anglers who equate subsurface fly life imitations with live bait are more correct than they mean to be. Aquatic insects in nymphal stages tend to be ugly-looking and, in some instances, almost nondescript. Trout streams harbor varied species of aquatic fly life in varied stages, so trout are furnished a plethora of sizes and shapes of subsurface foods (which supports the axiom that they feed 75 percent of the time beneath the surface, where there is less possibility of their feeding selectively). So the nymph and wet fly fisherman can subscribe to an "anything goes" approach and still expect to be successful, if he doesn't mind periodic snagging while fishing with weight. Once he's resigned to living with hang-ups, allows more time per stretch because of them, and concentrates on studying water, chances are good that he will develop "the nymph fisherman's feel." It's a safe bet, too, that in the long run he will take more trout by nymphing than by the other methods.

I asked George Harvey to begin his lessons with streamers since, because of their large size, most beginning fly tyers cut their teeth on them. A case can be made, though, for starting with nymphs, or attempting them very soon after streamers. For more than any other artificials, nymph imitations enable tyro tyers to convince themselves that their own offerings will catch trout!

The most effective streamers—beyond being attractors—should possess deceiving qualities, but their large size makes this a pretty big order. Even streamerettes look less like minnow or fry fish than wet and dry imitations resemble their natural counterparts. Dry flies should be tied exactingly enough to float realistically, but nymphs can be sloppily tied, awful-looking counterfeits, and they will very often take fish—many more than badly tied streamers or dry flies. Since the beginning tyer's first flies will usually be poorly made, it's my contention that the sooner he ties nymphs, the more quickly will he prove to himself that his vise's first products can be trout-takers.

Would that I had begun tying nymphs along with streamers! I forfeited untold enjoyment at the vise and on stream by avoiding them. When I discovered that bad ties were often as efficient as good ones, I embraced nymph fishing with fervor, hang-ups notwithstanding. As was the case with so much of my evolving knowledge of fly angling lore, John Stauffer was responsible.

John came naturally to his practical approach to fly fishing. Bred in the frugal, utilitarian traditions of his ancestor, Hans Herr—Lancaster County's first settler—John worked on his ancestral farm as a boy. He had worm-fished there, but after meeting fly fishermen in the Poconos he was quickly converted. One evening at a cocktail party (just after I got out of college) my father introduced me to John, saying, "Sam likes to fish. Maybe you could take him to the mountains sometime."

Poor John had no out! The following spring he dutifully invited me to his club for a weekend.

I had fooled around with flies on our family farm as a boy, after my grandfather stocked trout in a pond. But on that first Pocono outing I was thoroughly drilled in the fundamentals of fly fishing. John began by asking me to follow him in crossing the stream at a particularly rough, heavy stretch. I was knocked down. He then showed me how to wade in rough water. "The lesson won't be lost on you now that you've gone in," he said, laughing.

I caught one eight-inch brook trout on a Mickey Finn streamer and was hooked for life.

Shortly after our first trip to John's camp he taught me to tie flies. And during those first years of tying he often dropped by my house on winter evenings to supervise my work. Prerequisite equipment for John on these occasions was a fifth of Early Times bourbon. John's massive hulk would crowd the vise on the card table, scattered with rooster necks, bucktail, floss, and chenille, his rugged, intent visage—highlighted by lamplight—resembling that of Mount Rushmore's Jefferson, reflecting the beams of a setting sun. John reminded me on one particular evening that I'd been too long with streamers, that I should tie some wets and nymphs. When I said that I rarely used the damn things he replied that I should definitely try the one he was going to tie. He soon snapped the vise and dropped a mangy-looking wet fly on the table.

"Perla Capitita—stone fly," he said. "You fish it like a nymph, dead drift." Then he dipped the fly in his highball glass, dropped it on a sheet of white paper under the lamp's light and, literally drooling over the whiskey-drenched, unseemly looking morsel of counterfeit trout food, murmured with glee, "Doesn't it look succulent and deadly?" Over the years John used these words many times, always with reference to nymphs and wet flies. If they looked "succulent," they were "deadly."

He then urged me to try my hand on a Perla Capitita. Mine was not as well formed as John's, and I was chagrined. He told me to fill my glass and dip it in Early Times. As I dropped the dripping thing on the white paper I had to agree with John about its being pretty damn succulent and deadly after all. As the evening wore on and the level of whiskey dropped appreciably in the bottle, our Perla Capititas looked more and more alike and increasingly succulent and deadly.

When we finished I couldn't distinguish my ties from John's. And he was the expert! His flies murdered trout, so my mangy-looking things just could not fail!

John's tie was: Body: dark brown hare's-ear fur lightly mixed with dyed seal's fur. Wing case: barred flank feathers from mandarin drake, tied flat against body. Legs: grouse hackle. Tail: two short barbs from a cock pheasant tail. Hook size: 8 or 10, dark-red silk.

The Perla Capitita was deadly in the extreme at its first trial, and while this wet fly continued to produce well, there were no particularly spectacular experiences until a couple of years later when I was pond fishing for native brook trout in Quebec. My guide was a French Canadian teenager who was hopelessly addicted to wet Dark Montreals. His strategy was typical of the area: canoe trolling, punctuated by casting (to lessen the boredom) and deep jerking retrieves. Another hotel guest and I had rather spotty fishing with the Montreals, so I switched to John Stauffer's wonder fly. So did my partner, and we committed mayhem. In two days we supplied the hotel keeper with brookies sufficient for a dinner menu, and he was gratified enough to give us our last night's lodging free!

The Perla Capitita's great deadliness proved to be erratic over the years, but the Leadwing Coachman (nymph and wet) has been almost constant in its capacity to produce. The Leadwing seems to me one of the most reliable of flies under all conditions, everywhere. Some angler-entomologists attribute its effectiveness to its representing the Isonchia Bicolor, a May fly that hatches over an extended period, but I prefer John Stauffer's contention that it's one of the "buggiest"-looking of trout flies. ("Buggy" was another of John's pet descriptions for nymphs and wet flies.)

He demonstrated the fly's buggy appearance one winter evening, again through the medium of Early Times. I was fascinated when the almost sea-green peacock herl body, after a wetting, took on sickly emerald hues. "Disgusting-looking, isn't it?" said John, grinning. "As disgustingly realistic as a just-swatted fly on a clean white tablecloth!"

As long ago as the end of the nineteenth century G. E. M. Skues reported in his classic *The Way of a Trout with a Fly* that the Alder fly imitation (with a peacock herl body) was a most effective fly in England and on the continent. Frequently after I've drawn blanks on other patterns, the Leadwing has brought at least a modicum of action, so I'm convinced that this wet fly's (or nymph's) secret of success lies in its close resemblance to many honest-to-God insects. Thus, it's the best of all substitutes for live bait.

Segmented bodies are common to a wide variety of aquatic insect life at all stages of development. Many segmented imitations are almost dead ringers of naturals. At the risk of offending entomologically oriented exponents of exact imitations, I suggest that under some conditions exaggerated rather than true-to-life segmentations are more efficacious. Particularly in brisk currents and roiled water a fly's ability to exaggerate a natural's components—leg, tail, wing (or wing-case) segmentations—is very important. This contention seemed to be borne out by my experiences with the C. K. Nymph, the "anytime, anywhere" fly.

Early in the spring of 1970 Dr. Lever Stewart phoned me from Charlottesville, Virginia. We had not met since leaving school 28 years before. He had just read my book *Simplified Fly Fishing* and wanted to send his copy to me for autographing. He said that he had started fly fishing four years ago and that it was high time for a reunion on his favorite stream, the Jackson. I accepted his kind invitation for a weekend in early May.

I arrived in Charlottesville late Friday afternoon. Our jubilant meeting was followed by a visit to the nearby tackle shop, where Stewart introduced me to the owner-manager, Chuck

Kraft. Chuck, an inveterate fly angler, has an encyclopedic knowledge of the trout waters in western Virginia's Highland and Bath counties.

Lever and I agreed to meet Chuck early the next morning at Monterey, 90 miles away, but a long night of reminiscing resulted in a late start, so we didn't get to Monterey until long after Chuck had left for the Jackson. During our long drive over the Alleghenies, Lever told me about the wonders of a nymph that Chuck had concocted. It was, he said, a tried-and-true stand-by of fly fishermen in the area, and it produced consistently when other flies did not. Now I'd been fly fishing for so many years that naturally I expressed some doubt. But Stewart was insistent—so much so, in fact, that he stopped the car and dug a C. K. (Chuck Kraft) Nymph from his fly box. "Looks like a Woolly Worm," I commented. "Don't say that to Chuck," Lever said. "He gets burned up when people make the comparison."

When we began fishing a sparse hatch of Quill Gordons was on the water. Trout were not rising well to it. Our matching artificials brought little action and no fish. Lever urged that I try Chuck's pattern. When I agreed, he put his rod down and readied a camera.

"Now we'll get some action, and I want to prove it," he said.

I delivered the nymph upstream to a gentle, riffled glide and permitted a dead drift return. There was no take. The second cast, farther up, failed to produce. The third went to white water at the glide's head. The nymph washed into deep water along the far bank, on my right. Halfway down it stopped, and I tightened line. My six-foot fiberglass fly rod telegraphed hammerlike thumps, and a foot-long rainbow trout sped upstream and tail-walked through the white water. When I pressured him slightly, he coursed rapidly back to deep water.

Lever alternated shutter clicks with excited "told you so's." After I dropped back to the tail of the glide and netted my fish, he literally pushed me up to the next stretch. The performance was repeated twice, with 10- and 8-inch rainbows, respectively.

Rather sheepishly I joined my exultant partner at bankside and admitted that the C. K. Nymph might be pretty good. By way of testing it, I suggested that he fish the C. K. while I tried a Leadwing Coachman nymph.

Although the river was not high for early spring, it flowed full and strong. Even though the day was sunny and warm, recent cold weather and spring-fed inlets kept water temperatures in the mid to high 50s. Conditions plainly favored subsurface feeding. What with strong currents and the fact that my fish had all struck in deep water, weighted nymphs seemed definitely in order. All of Chuck Kraft's were tied lead wire. So I chose a leaded Coachman.

Over the next hour I enjoyed good action. But the half-dozen trout I landed were small, while Lever caught larger trout—an even dozen. Of course, he knew the water better than I, but even so, his fly was clearly giving him an advantage.

At 2:00 P.M. Chuck Kraft joined us for a streamside lunch. Since 7:00 A.M. he had caught more than 25 trout on his nymph and had kept three.

After lunch, while the others fished, I meandered along the river, took pictures and reveled in the springtime verdure of Allegheny ridges. As the sun turned brassy and shadows darkened the river's tea-colored glides, I went back to fishing. With increased fly hatching, surface action picked up. I fished dry with more success. But trout were in the six- to eight-inch range. So, I soon went back to the C. K. Nymph and scored a very lucky victory over a big brownie Lever had raised a couple of times earlier, fought, and lost.

After dinner in Monterey we asked Chuck to join us in our motel room so that I could quiz him in more detail about his wonder nymph. He had experimented with between 40 and 50 color combinations, but by far the most effective were his two original patterns. One had a body of black wool and the other was charcoal gray. Hook shanks were first wrapped with .025 lead wire. Tails were lemon wood duck. Hackle was grizzly—Palmer-tied and clipped. His original ties were made on Mustad 3X long hooks, 9762. Chuck fishes varying sizes of the black and gray patterns; more often than not he used size 8. I took the large brown trout on a No. 8 but got most of my action on a No. 10. Chuck said No. 12s and 14s are very effective for low-water fishing late in the season.

Why was the nymph so deadly? "I tried to get the general appearance of a cross section of nymphs," Chuck explained, "say, that of stone flies, hellgrammites, even case caddis and some May flies.

"Against the current it can look minnowlike," he added. "And when those many hackle points pulsate in the flow, they can attract fish."

His nymphs have been fished extensively in the Eastern states as far south as southern Georgia, west to Michigan, Wyoming, Montana, and up in the Northwest Territories of Canada. They're great fish-takers everywhere and have also been used successfully for bass, bluegills, crappies, rock bass, pickerel, and yellow perch.

I had a chance to further test the "anywhere, anytime" nature of the fly a little later when our family was in Denver, Colorado, for my oldest daughter's graduation. During our five-day stay I met Pete Van Gytenbeck, then Executive Director of Trout, Unlimited. Pete invited me and my associate, Ralph Mille, to stay at his camp on the Platte River for a weekend of trout fishing. The spring runoff in the Rockies was late, and the river was high. The water was difficult to read. Obstructions were so deep that the river looked like an irrigation ditch.

Since Pete was unable to accompany us and we were unfamiliar with the area, our only alternative was to fish our way downriver with large streamers. Two hours of streamer quar-

tering brought no action. At last we found a fishy-looking spot
—a hairpin turn in the middle of which was a dry gravel bar.
Ralph got a couple of passes from a foot-long brown trout that
didn't connect. Then I took a 10-inch rainbow.

"Now that we've located some fish," I told Ralph, "I'll show
you how well my wonder nymph will take 'em."

I angled a quartering cast downstream to the gravel's fall-
off, fed line, and let it sink at midstream. The line tightened,
and I struck. A geyser of white water erupted as a rainbow that
had to go 20 inches vaulted out and up. Even though this big
fish threw the hook, I was elated and called to Ralph, "I told
you so!"

"Let's see that thing," he said excitedly.

We sat down on the bank, and I told him the story of the C.
K. Nymph. When I was done, I laughed at myself. I must have
appeared as excited to Ralph as Lever Stewart had to me—and
I'd been fly fishing for almost a quarter of a century. But that's
what happens when you find a fly which will work its wonders
anytime and anywhere.

Sometimes during our fly-tying sessions John Stauffer, in
reminiscing about fishing with the late Jim Leisenring, dwelt
on how beautifully (and successfully) this famous wet fly
fisherman drifted night crawlers. He cast them far upstream
and, using a hand-twist retrieve, guided them faultlessly
around rocks, into glides, through eddying pockets, along
bankside cuts into pools. No purist, Jim Leisenring used whatever conditions called for, and this sometimes (particularly
after a rain squall) was a big, succulent night crawler. Under
Jim's influence John fished wet flies in the same manner, the
theory being that hatching or sunken flies will ride the same
currents as night crawlers, or any trout food for that matter.

Taking this wet fly strategy for gospel, I aped John. But
much angling literature revealed the surprising fact that wet
flies should be quartered against the current, like streamers.

John contended that this traditional method stemmed from the early days of fly angling when the exigencies of equipment dictated downstream presentation and that this didn't make sense. Still, most of the fly anglers I met on stream fished wet flies in the traditional manner. This was true of members of a club I joined in the Poconos. But my wet flies fished upstream usually took more fish than those quartered against the current by my companions.

Once when Maury Delman (then editor of *Fishing World* magazine) was my guest our dead-drifted wet flies outshone the classically fished wets of a graybeard club member to the extent that he became peeved. "You're not doing it right, Sam," he said later. "You fished wet flies like goddamned nymphs, and conditions don't call for 'em!"

Being a respecter of age, I avoided reminding my friend that Maury and I caught fish and he didn't. But I could not resist opining that he fished wet flies like g.-d. streamers, and conditions didn't call for them, either! Water was low. So while nymphs would surely have worked, there seemed little need to fish them since we had no need to "go deep" and risk snagging. There were sparse and scattered hatches of May and stone flies. But trout were not surface-feeding. Plainly, wet fly imitations of *hatching* nymphs had been in order.

This experience prompted Maury Delman to team up with me on an article for *Sports Afield*, titled "Are Wet Fly Fishermen All Wet?" The volume of mail resembled that which might follow the discovery of the proverbial missing link. And it came from fly fishermen! Only one fellow took the "so what else is new?" line. He had fished wet upstream for years, as indeed have others—W. C. Stuart and G. E. M. Skues being among the most noted—over a long period. But the interest aroused by the development of "flymphs" by V. S. (Pete) Hiedy, as well as the writings of Doug Swisher and Carl Richards on emerging flies (fished in the surface film), indicates it's time for generally accepted wet fly practice to be updated so that anglers can benefit from advances made in tackle technology.

It's necessary to go into this subject because upstream presentation renders the wet fly anything but passé, as some anglers claim it to be by virtue of the evolution of streamers and nymphs. For as flymphs (or emerging nymphs), wet flies can be fished a lot, if not most of the time, very rewardingly. Thus, fly tyers who include more wet flies in their repertoire have more latitude for craft improvement. My own experiences with wet flies bears this out.

By the end of our first July in a cottage we have rented in the Poconos for some years now I began to realize that midsummer conditions were conducive to more than the hit-or-miss fishing of "junk." How I used to wish that the superb evening hatches and spinner falls of June would continue through July! With the coming of dog days trout turned somnolent, until disturbed (which they so easily were) in shriveled glides, shallow flats, and glassy pools. It was difficult to know what kind of flies they would take. There was always a wide variety of naturals around, but nothing would seem to predominate. This caused a lack of predictability and rhythm to rises. They were sporadic, now and again, here and there. The odd high jump under a rhododendron bush—was he after a dangling inchworm? A belly flash against golden gravel— some nymphing, no doubt. An occasional surface bulge— hatching nymphs for sure! A dimple in a glide—maybe a floating ant caused it. And then—all too seldom—a spectacular surface take of an emerging dun or a falling spinner. A miss on such a rise was enough to drive me to the swimming pool with a book, sweating and cursing my luck for getting the damn cottage in July! But a more positive view revealed that the junk inhabiting streams in July could be represented by a veritable smorgasbord of counterfeits, the tempting of

44

trout with which was bound to make for more sophisticated practices on stream and at my vise.

A midsummer dry fly of great effectiveness here is a small black caddis fly. I imitated it with a size No. 16 dry Black Gnat. Before we had the cottage I fished it a lot on summer weekends with great success. In keen anticipation of the next season I would invariably tie too many during the winter. Had I tied "junk" instead—varied sizes of dries, wets, nymphs, and terrestrials—and been more observant of conditions calling for the use of each, I would have had a more enjoyable vacation. For it was a sure thing that a No. 16 dry Black Gnat couldn't produce well full time! So during the winter of 1965–66 I began a tying program for the following July. For the first time I attempted a varied assortment of terrestrials, midges, small wet flies, and nymphs. A killer for the nymph stage of that small black stone fly, for instance, turned out to be a wet No. 16 Leadwing Coachman with a black, rather than a gray, wing, or wing case. I also tied flymph patterns of midsummer May flies such as Cahills, Ginger Quills, and my worshipful Leadwing Coachman.

For deep pools over trout's siestas, I worked on large Muskrat, C. K., and Leadwing nymphs. And I tied many nymphs and wet renditions of tiny (No. 18 to 20) Sulphur May flies, the better to match emerging naturals, common here during July evenings. I was tying for late afternoon when these small flies —getting ready to hatch—provide just-below-the-surface trout fare. These nymphs and wets really rang the bell when I used them an hour or two before quitting time! The dry stage was, of course, terrific later, on those evenings when I could shake the family.

Ever since the summer of 1966 I've enjoyed July's junk fishing in the Poconos. So much so, ironically, that I now fish wet as much, or more, in dog days as in early spring, the generally accepted time for subsurface trouting.

45

Arnold Gingrich, in his charming *Joys of Trout* (Crown), comes across as the only angler observant (and honest) enough to question the ancient aphorism about trout angling being a contemplative sport:

> More often than not the thoughts of an angler, at least while he's actually fishing, would be overpriced at a penny. The angler's mind, while making those countless casts, is so often lulled by the repetitive motion that he is reduced to a state of suspended mental animation, a trancelike level of slowed-down activity, that is the next thing to that suspension of thought induced by sleep. That's why I could never really see the aptness of old Izaak's rather pretentious tag for it as "the contemplative man's recreation." Walton was, obviously, a most exceptional man, but I still think that his real "contemplating" was done at home, with purposive intent, in his study, rather than on the banks of the Dove.

I was greatly relieved on reading this the other evening. For many years I believed that I somehow must be "different." Where, when, how—I used to ask myself—can one become contemplative while fly fishing? The bait fisher's lot, of course, *is* a contemplative one. What else is there to do but dreamily wait for the cork to bob? The exigencies of fly angling, however, dictate constant observance of surroundings. Indeed, you're often downright busy. When I come in, hell, I come in beat—happy, to be sure, but beat. Maybe I try to cover too much water. There is always that next stretch or pool just upstream to sample before quitting time.

Further ruminations on the subject, however, led me to the conclusion that fly angling can become "the contemplative man's recreation," for the seeds of contemplation *do* exist for the *tying angler* in the form of his flies themselves. Sometimes when changing flies the sight of a particular pattern in my box gives rise to memories of its fabrication. I can't attach a Little Brown Trout streamer to a leader without remembering the snow-filled night of its prototype's birth. These 11 years of

46

Julys, during which I've rediscovered wet flies, have afforded many opportunities for meditation, because when varied patterns are dressed over a given winter, it's easier during the following season to single out individual flies and mark in memory the evenings when they were tied.

Certain recollections of seemingly innocuous winter-evening interludes, often in the living room with my family, have prompted misgivings about my lack of progress in fly tying. My flies aren't the better for these many years at the vise. They lack distinction, a certain refinement, which precludes their exhibition at anglers' gatherings. The really tough, minute terrestrial ties had been so bad that I gave up on them.

I remember angler-author Don DuBois's injunction after I'd denigrated one of my May fly midges a few years ago: "You can't tie well at a card table in the living room with the children and a German shepherd. There's no incentive to strive for perfection, and that's what tying is all about."

Another remark, by a friend about John Stauffer, came to mind: "Johnny was a bad influence on your tying. All his life he tied flies with a bottle of whiskey and his stuff looked ratty. Johnny made you lazy at the vise!"

Yes, I'd been a lazy fly tyer. Incongruous, for I worked hard at my fishing and writing. Then, while staring into the crystal depths of a rock-lined pocket, truth's light dawned. So what if it was impossible to ruminate about the pleasures of fly angling while in the act? I'd done so at home—like "old Izaak" —during winter evenings. And without "purposive intent"! Better that meditations on the joys of angling (or the joys of trout!) impede my progress at the card table rather than on the stream! So I vowed to remain a lazy fly tyer, the better to experience the contemplative side of fly angling, the pleasures of which are so difficult to savor onstream. But if you're willing to try now and again, on a streamside boulder, you will find (as I often have) that the expenditure of only a little time can result in sharpened faculties and the ability to fish more expectantly.

I can't resist noting—with all due respects to Mr. Gingrich's perceptive observations—that beyond being therapeutic and an outlet for creative instincts, the tying of one's own flies gives form to one's angling ruminations. Or better, lends them some degree of perspective, to the end that "tying anglers" can say with "old Izaak" that angling *is* the contemplative man's recreation—and really mean it!

NYMPHS

Nymphs are probably the easiest fly for a beginner to tie, because of their simplicity.

First one must learn how to hold and tie on the tail material. This is illustrated by Diagram #1. The tail should be about one third as long

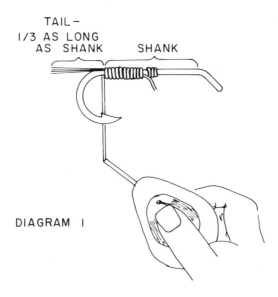

TAIL —
1/3 AS LONG
AS SHANK   SHANK

DIAGRAM I

as the hook shank. Now carefully study the illustrations. Attach tying thread to hook as illustrated in drawing. Wind tying thread almost back to bend of hook. Now hold tail material as illustrated. The holding procedure is one of the most important in fly tying. It is used when any material is tied to a hook. Diagram #2 (a), (b) and (c) illustrates the steps. Practice holding tail material until your angle of grasp is such that the tail material will lay flat on top of shank. Now lay tail on top of shank so that the ends will be about one third longer than the shank. Bring tying thread up between thumb and tail material. Be sure to bring thread back far enough between thumb and tail so it can be held

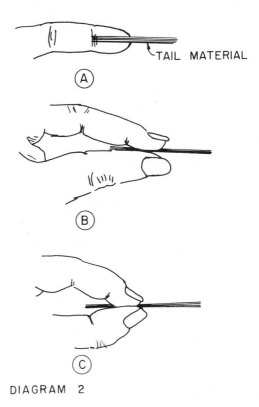

TAIL MATERIAL

(A)

(B)

(C)

DIAGRAM 2

securely when finger and thumb are squeezed together as in (b). Wind thread over top of tail, then down opposite side between finger and tail. Before you draw tying thread up tight close thumb and finger as in (c). Squeeze firmly and draw tying thread tight by pulling gently but firmly down. Now hold tying thread tight and make several more turns of tying thread around tail material until thread is back at the bend of the hook.

Diagram #3: After tail is secured take small piece of tinsel, gold or silver wire and tie in at bend of hook. Take some dubbing material (fur from any animal, with guard hairs pulled out and mixed by pulling apart and placing back together again until no bunches are present).

50

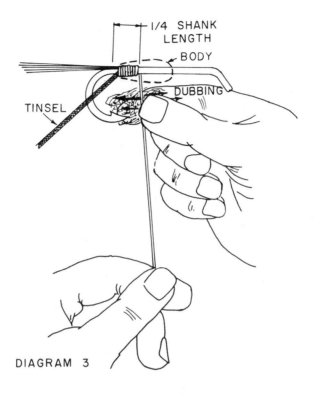

1/4 SHANK LENGTH

BODY

DUBBING

TINSEL

DIAGRAM 3

Hold tying thread taut with left hand, three or four inches below shank of hook. Take a little fur (sparse) between thumb and finger of right hand and lay it on underside of tying thread close to shank of hook. The index finger, at first joint, should be placed on the underside of the thread to hold the dubbing in place. Now place thumb as diagrammed, squeeze firmly, and spin on dubbing by movement of thumb and finger as diagrammed. Start winding dubbed body. Keep adding dubbing if necessary in same manner until you have enough to build the body halfway to the eye of the hook. Finished abdomen should be shape of the dotted line. Next spiral the ribbing material (tinsel) up to end of abdomen, and tie off.

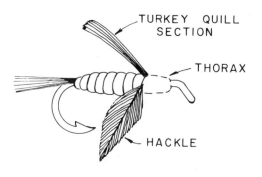

TURKEY QUILL
SECTION

THORAX

HACKLE

DIAGRAM 4

Diagram #4: Take a section of turkey-wing quill, fold together and tie in as diagrammed. Now tie in hackle. Spin more dubbing on thread and build up thorax as illustrated by dotted line. Now wind four turns of hackle in front of abdomen and tie off. Cut off hackle fibers from top and bottom so only ones on sides remain. Pull the turkey section over top of thorax, hold tight, and tie off back of eye of hook. Cut off excess and then make several turns of tying thread to build up the head. Secure by half hitches or whip finish. Cut off thread and apply laquer to head.

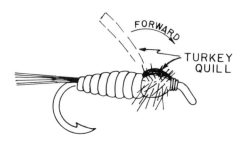

FORWARD

TURKEY
QUILL

DIAGRAM 5

Diagram 5: This is a simple nymph, and if you tie up a few dozen with light, medium, and dark dubbing on #s 10, 12, 14, 16 hooks, you should have no trouble taking trout anyplace you fish.

If you wish to weight the nymph bodies, lead wire should be wound on before the preceding operations. It is suggested you use three different diameters of wire (.020 light), (.028 medium), (.032 heavy). This will give you a good range of nymphs for all types of water. I use different colored tying thread at the head to indicate the amount of weight used (yellow for light, green for medium, and black for heavy). This makes it easier to select the correct weighted nymph as water conditions change.

SUGGESTED NYMPH PATTERNS

Name	Head	Tail	Ribbing	Body	Hackle	Wing
Stone Fly Creeper	blue dun horns	stripped brown hackle quills	fine gold tinsel	gray-brown fur or wool	brown turkey fiber legs	gray turkey
Leadwing Coach-man	black	brown hackle barbules		peacock herl	brown legs	small slate
Hendrick-son	light gray	wood duck		gray-green fur	blue dun	small light slate
Light Cahill	cream	wood duck		cream wool	light ginger	small mallard breast
Muskrat (Harvey)		black hackle	silver wire	black dyed muskrat	black	black goose quill section (folded)

WET FLIES WITH WINGS

    After one has tied several dozen bucktails and nymphs as previously described, the wet fly should be fairly easy to tie.

    Diagram # 1: Attach tying thread and wind back to bend of hook, tie in tail as diagrammed. Be sure tail is held so it is on top of shank. The tail should extend back from the bend as long as the hook shank.

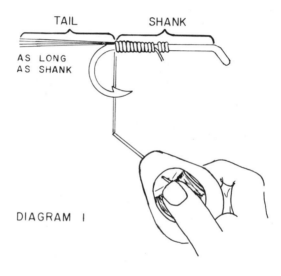

    For this fly we will use floss for the body; but dubbed fur, quill, chenille, or tinsel bodies may be used. We are just using the floss for a body so the tyer gets used to using different materials.

    Diagram #2: After tail, tie in small piece of floss (about six inches long) at bend of hook and then wind tying thread up to one-fourth distance back of eye. Now start winding body. Be sure the first turn of floss at bend of hook does not bend tail material down over back side of hook.

54

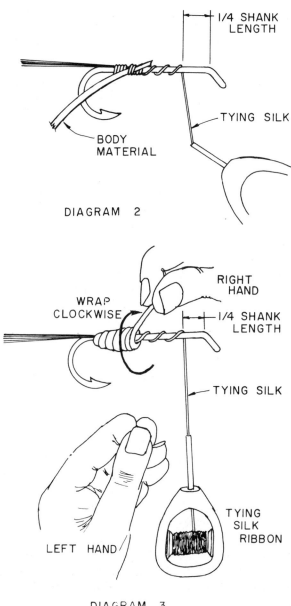

1/4 SHANK LENGTH

TYING SILK

BODY MATERIAL

DIAGRAM 2

WRAP CLOCKWISE

RIGHT HAND

1/4 SHANK LENGTH

TYING SILK

TYING SILK RIBBON

LEFT HAND

DIAGRAM 3

Diagram #3: When winding on body material, use the right hand to take the material over top of shank and the left hand to pick it up on the underside. Try to build a tapered body as in Diagram #4. Sometimes you must wind back over the body to build up more bulk or to get a better taper. When doing this make sure to keep each wrap close together, otherwise you will find the body material coming loose.

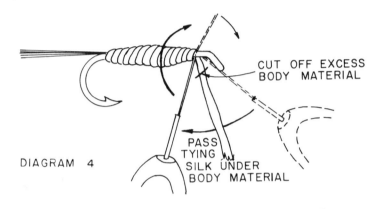

CUT OFF EXCESS BODY MATERIAL

PASS TYING SILK UNDER BODY MATERIAL

DIAGRAM 4

Now select a good soft hackle that is the correct size for the hook you are using. First strip off the lower third of the fibers from the quill. This will make it much easier to tie off the hackle. Now stroke back fibers between thumb and index finger, working from tip to stump end.

Diagram #5: Tie in tip end of hackle with the bottom, or dull side facing the body. Be sure to make enough turns to secure tip. Cut off protruding tip end. Attach hackle pliers to stump end of quill and start winding on hackle so that dull side faces the tail end of the fly. The first turn should be tight against the body and each succeeding turn tight against the previous turn. After each turn it is a good idea to stroke the fibers back by using the thumb and first two fingers of the left hand. When you have made three to five turns of hackle, hold and tie off as in Diagram #6. Be sure not to crowd the eye. Cut off hackle quill and make several more turns to secure hackle.

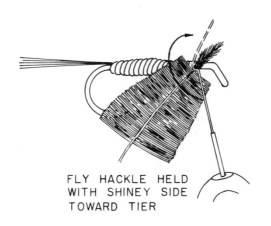

FLY HACKLE HELD
WITH SHINEY SIDE
TOWARD TIER

DIAGRAM 5

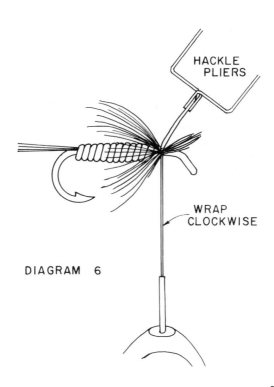

HACKLE
PLIERS

WRAP
CLOCKWISE

DIAGRAM 6

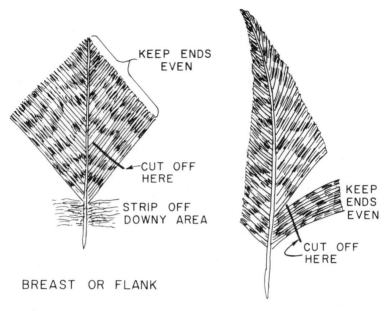

KEEP ENDS
EVEN

CUT OFF
HERE

STRIP OFF
DOWNY AREA

KEEP
ENDS
EVEN

CUT OFF
HERE

BREAST OR FLANK

DIAGRAM 7

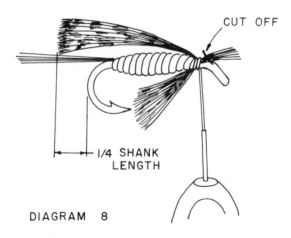

CUT OFF

1/4 SHANK
LENGTH

DIAGRAM 8

Now look over Diagrams #7 and #8. Select flank or breast feathers from mallard or other duck and cut out section for wing. This is held between thumb and finger of left hand and is tied on top as diagrammed, using the same method as you used when tying in the tail.

The wing should be about a fourth longer than the hook. Most beginners have a tendency to make the wing too long. After the wing is secured, cut off excess, take enough winds of tying thread to cover all the material, and make a smooth head. Secure with half hitches or whip finish. A drop of lacquer on the head and the fly is finished!

Diagrams # 9, 10, 11 show the steps in tying a wet fly using matched quill sections for wings. You may select matching wing quills from any bird, if the fibers are long enough for the size fly you are tying. However, duck, turkey, and goose quills will be the easiest for the beginner to use.

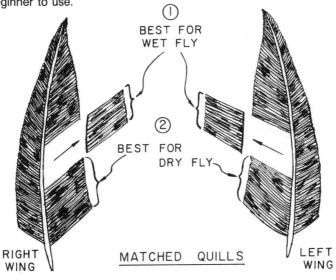

① BEST FOR WET FLY

② BEST FOR DRY FLY

RIGHT WING

LEFT WING

MATCHED QUILLS

DIAGRAM 9

Study Diagram #9. Then select two matching quills and cut a section from each quill. The width of the quill sections should be about three fourths as wide as the gap of the hook you are tying on. Moisten finger and thumb (I use my tongue) of the right hand and place thumb and finger on quill sections as shown in Diagram #10. Moisture will hold sections. You may have to make some adjustments in angle of grasp so that the two sections lay evenly together when you close your thumb and finger. Lay over top of the hook to gauge the right length. Then grasp between thumb and finger of left hand as illustrated in

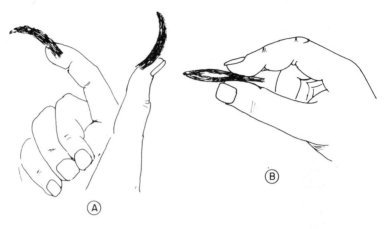

DIAGRAM 10

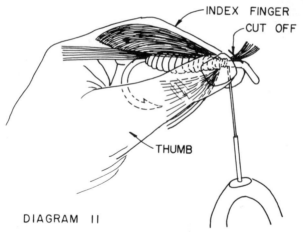

INDEX FINGER
CUT OFF

THUMB

DIAGRAM 11

Diagram #11. Note the thumb and finger straddle the shank of the hook and the wings lie flat on top of the body. The tips of the thumb and finger, when closed, should extend to, or slightly beyond, the eye of the hook. All other operations are the same as described for the flank feather section wing.

Name	Head	Tail	Ribbing	Body	Tip	Hackle	Wing
Iron-Blue Dun	black	furnace hackle barbules		blue-gray fur or wool	scarlet floss	furnace	slate
Cow-dung	black			olive-green wool or floss	gold tinsel	brown	cin-namon
Hare's Ear	black	brown hackle barbules	gold tinsel	hare's-ear fur		hare's-ear fur	gray mallard quill or brown turkey
March Brown	black	brown par-tridge	flat gold tinsel	olive-brown wool		brown par-tridge	brown turkey
Alder	black			pea-cock herl	gold tinsel	black	brown turkey

3. "On Young Flies, Before They Are Able to Flie Awaie, Do Fish Feed Exceedingly"

—JOHN TAVERNER, 1600

PERHAPS BECAUSE OF their close proximity to New England, some Adirondack fly anglers favor traditional Yankee methods—namely, the quartered fishing of classic wet fly patterns with little emphasis on the imitating of specific insect hatches—a practice brought to pass, no doubt, by the propensity of native brook trout ("square-tails" in New England) to be naïvely more prone to attractor flies than deceivers. Since New England's wilderness areas remained in a virgin state later than those of the Catskills and Poconos, it was natural for the wily, imported European brown trout to take over from his less sophisticated American cousin first in New York and Pennsylvania, whose major trout streams have since been dubbed "the cradle of the dry fly in America."

Sam Black personifies his durable Scots-Irish ancestors who wrested central Pennsylvania from the red men during the French and Indian War. A much decorated combat soldier in World War II who boxed for the Fleet Marines, Sam preserves his wiry, tough-as-leather physique by extended wilderness treks, trying enough to scare the shorts off today's average back-packer. In the course of doing odd jobs in the Adirondacks over prewar summers, he took up fly fishing and developed into a typical Adirondack fly angler of the old school. First he concentrated on bass fishing, the only trout he took being from woodland rivulets during camping excursions. Occasionally he returned to the Adirondacks to fish deep in the boondocks for native brookies. I could never interest Sam in brown trout, hatch matching, or fly tying. His few old Adirondack patterns served his limited purposes.

By way of broadening Sam's outlook, I took him to the Poconos in early June a couple of years ago. Much to my chagrin the weather was atrocious; fly hatches were practically nonexistent, and there was no surface feeding. He had never fished upstream, but early in his first attempt he took a 16-inch stream-bred brownie on one of my C. K. nymphs. Sam was amazed at the slow take.

"That's because for the first time in your life you've fooled a trout—not just excited him into striking!" I said, apparently making my point. For at our meetings during the following year Sam referred to the incident frequently, allowing that he would like to try fooling 'em some more—on dry flies.

Our next June weekend was a hatch-matcher's delight. At about 7:30 of the first evening light Cahills began to emerge. We fished rises quite successfully until 8:15, when I called Sam off the stream to explain what was turning out to be a rare and exciting phenomenon. While the Cahill hatch continued unabetted, small Sulphurs, fresh from their mating dances overhead, began to touch down to lay their eggs. Stretches that dimpled previously now boiled. In 25 years of fishing this stream I could not recall a rise of trout to equal this one. Sam retained a Cahill, and I went to a spent-wing Sulphur, size #18. We took turns "calling our shots" and caught and released perhaps a dozen nice trout between us over the next half hour. Darkness and low-flying bats drove us off the stream about nine o'clock.

The next evening brought incipient cloudiness and humidity. Wispy tendrils of light fog wound through massive stands of hemlocks surrounding the glen pool. Here the stream's largest trout abide. I hoped that Sam might tie into one come the evening hatch, but come it did not—nor did many spinners fall. There was no surface activity.

We lounged at the pool's tail from 7:00 until 8:00 P.M., when a concurrent but sparse hatch of three flies commenced—light Cahills, little Sulphurs, and Yellow Sally stone flies. Hard against the solid-rock lining of the pool's far side, three quarters of the way up, a trout began to rise. Hugging the wall, he gently sipped in flies floating almost flush to the wall. Those riding a foot or two beyond the wall were ignored. Being about 35 to 40 feet distant, we could not determine the fish's size or whether he was being selective.

I showed Sam three imitations of the naturals and suggested that he try the Cahill. He insisted that what with all my talk about hatch-matching, it was fitting that *I* demonstrate. I got off an adequate cast, and the No. 14 Cahill floated neatly to the fish, but there was no take. Two more near perfect drifts would not move him.

Crooking the rod under my left arm, I switched to a No. 18 little Sulphur. Again, I was able to get the range, and the fly began to eddy and drift against the wall. As it neared the strike zone, I tensed, raised my left arm, and pointed out the bobbing Sulphur. With the gentlest of sips, the trout took it.

There was no screaming of the reel, eruptings of white water, or echoing fall-backs. And I couldn't have cared less about the trout's measuring a bare 10 inches. For I'd stood in the stream and "found the answer" with a home-tied fly, much to the edification of my doubting sidekick. No more fish rose, but we lingered until darkness enveloped the glen, and Sam, a birdwatcher, pointed out a phoebe describing erratic half rolls and chandelles overhead in a spirited quest for duns and spinners. Surely there's never been a more speedy conversion than Sam's. Intrigued by the concept of duping fish selectively with surface counterfeits, he relished the idea of some winter-tide tying sessions—just like mine with John Stauffer. We vowed to make a yearly pilgrimage to the stream to test our wares.

I shall always have fond memories of that evening. For besides experiencing high glee in playing the successful show-off, there was great satisfaction in introducing a typical some-time angler to fly tying. And, very important, the episode reminded me that there are very real obstacles to be overcome by beginning fly tyers seeking success with their first dry flies. I was prompted to reflect on my own problems and how they were overcome.

Art Flick's excellent *Streamside Guide* was literally that for me when I began seriously to pursue the tying of dries. And an excellent guide it was, too, in introducing me to the impor-tant May fly naturals and their imitations. My difficulties be-gan when I tried to identify the naturals on stream. I had no trouble with the Quill Gordon because of its early and almost solitary emergence on Eastern waters; but from the Hendrick-son's arrival to the end of the trout season it seemed next to impossible to single out a given fly, identify its genus, and dig in my fly box for the correct artificial. This is not to say that my Art Flick dries (and others) didn't score. They did. I simply was in the dark about exactly *what* I was trying to imitate. Naturally, during heavy hatches I attempted to match predominating colors and sizes, sometimes with great success. When fishing with partners experienced in fly identification I got on better, probably because I was confident that their chosen artificials would be the correct ones. But most of the time a lack of confidence in my ability to match naturals bred a lack of confidence in my ties themselves. Were they really tied to ride the surface properly? Did they sink too easily? Were they as close as possible in configuration to naturals?

Central to my difficulty was a malady peculiar to tyro an-gler-tyers that is best described as "Dry Fly Mesmerism." It's particularly catching, I submit, to those who dip too deeply into angling literature too soon.

"You don't learn fishing from a book," wrote Sparse Grey Hackle in the Foreword to my *Simplified Fly Fishing*, "you learn it from a fish." Here's an injunction every bit as valid as the old saw about a little knowledge being a dangerous thing. For while instructional literature can be very helpful to beginners, they will do better—once they've absorbed the basic "do's" and "don'ts"—to learn from the fish and his environment. More sophisticated writings should be read for vicarious pleasure. In large measure this is their *raison d'être*, a fact also succinctly noted by Sparse Grey Hackle. "The best fishing is in print."

There are, however, certain monumental and classic works bespeaking technological breakthroughs which can have a downright debilitating effect on a beginning tyer–hatch matcher's development. Since so much good angling literature is concerned with hatch matching, he's often prone to believe that success with dries will be in direct ratio to his knowledge of insect life. In the long run this is true, but it should be remembered that experienced angler-authors are writing for their peer group, who know when and where careful attention to entomological detail is necessary. Caught up in the unfamiliar and rarefied idiom of experienced hatch matchers, the neophyte is likely to put too great a premium on the close imitating of naturals. In a word, he can become mesmerized by the mystique of the dry fly to the extent of losing confidence in his ability to tie catching dry flies.

On some occasions I've attended fly anglers' conclaves and workshops with sometime fly fishermen and beginners who, after hearing their experienced brethren's declamations on hatch matching (replete with Latin terminology), developed inferiority complexes of sufficient magnitude to discourage them from fishing dry, let alone tying their own dry flies. I've become convinced that dry fly mesmerism is largely responsi-

66

ble for frightening away many potential converts to fly angling and tying.

But the syndrome can be kicked when the would-be hatch matcher proves to himself (as in case of nymphs, wets, and streamers) that his dry ties can get results. His first step must be to learn to tie dry flies that will float. The bivisible is without question the answer. By virtue of its construction it's the best possible floater *and* the simplest of flies to tie. A trip I took in mid-spring 1962 with beginning fly angler Dick Sherbahn graphically illustrates both points.

The start of our trip boded ill for its remainder. After getting off late, we had car trouble. Due to a mix-up in motel reservations, we arrived on the stream in midafternoon rather than early morning. What was worse, I forgot my dry fly box in the confusion. The box I had contained a smattering of wet flies, nymphs, and streamers. Dick urged me not to waste time by going back to the motel for my dries, so we fished wet all afternoon and had little action. A bright sun was beginning to weaken noticeably when Dick sloshed dejectedly up to a boulder where I sat smoking and mulling over a possible next move. I read in his glance presumption that insect imitating might just be a lot of malarkey. I told him to wait for sunset, when surface takes were a sure thing.

In minutes I came up with a start. A large cinnamon-colored May fly was fluttering overhead. Dick murmured something about one swallow's not making a summer. I replied that one March brown could make an evening. For one usually portends more of these big, succulent flies.

Above the ear-caressing song of riffles we heard the first rise, about 50 feet upstream in the lavender shadows of a deep-cut bank. We quickly switched to March brown wet flies in hopes that the trout might be hungry enough to take them for naturals about to hatch. But they didn't want them underwater. The varnishlike patina on gentle glides erupted white as the trout cleared water and came down on floating flies.

"They want 'em high and dry only," I told Dick disgustedly. "We've just got to get something to float!"

In desperation I fell back on an unfamiliar expedient. We hurried to the car and dug out an emergency fly-tying kit— unused since I'd prepared it for just such an occasion a few years before. I wound thread to the rear of a No. 12 hook and tied in three hackle feathers. After the thread was wrapped forward, I wound the hackle feathers forward also, tying each down with the thread. The fly was then whip-knotted into place behind the eye of the hook. I quickly tied three more. The result was a bushy mass of protruding hackle fibers. With no body to weight them, the fibers could "stand" on water, especially after being dunked in fly dressing. Luckily, I had some.

The sun was an orange smear when we got back to fishing. Fortunately, trout were still rising. One, in particular, interested us. He was working in a quiet slick under a footbridge, where each of his splashing reentries echoed loud and clear. As I was stripping line, two golf carts rolled off an adjoining course, and when the golfers piled out at the footbridge, our fish stopped rising.

Dick and I swapped pained glances. Then we broke out laughing at the utter futility of our trip.

"We're really star-crossed. . . ." Dick stopped in mid-sentence. The men on the bridge were signaling us. Amazingly, the fish was still in position.

"Throw your bait in here," one called. We didn't expect anything from that spooked trout. But Dick urged that I try out my bundle of hackle. So I slid a side-arm cast at the bridge, checking the line short of it so that only the leader alighted underneath. My fly floated cockily on the limpid, sun-reddened slick. Slowly, it drifted into the tail of the stretch.

"He's backing up!" yelled one of the golfers, whose view was unimpaired by the sun. Then we saw the trout, an airborne thing of beauty, contorting into a headlong plunge on the fly. Three towering leaps followed by a wild rush upstream failed to unseat the barb. To the cheers of the onlookers I was able to net this 13-inch deep-girthed brownie.

"Let's get out of here while we're ahead," I muttered to Dick, knowing well that our luck would never hold for more grandstanding. We moved on.

Purple shadows were deepening fast now, but trout were still splashing. And to the plaintive song of crickets, we took them almost at will. Darkness and the unraveling of my jerry-tied flies brought a successful end to a frustrating day. Between us we kept six trout, ranging from 11 to 14 inches.

Dick unjustly credited me with especial expertise because of that streamside fly-tying episode. Actually, I consider such tying a waste of time (for all except fools who forget their gear!). The truth is, Dick owed his success to the bivisible dry fly. As noted, not only is it the easiest dry fly to tie, as I proved, but it has qualities that make it easy to use and very lethal to boot.

The bivisible was a brainchild of the late Edward Ringwood Hewitt, one of the pioneer greats of American fly fishing. More than half a century of worldwide trouting provided Mr. Hewitt ample opportunity for *Telling on the Trout,* the title of his book. Some of his methods were ingenious, particularly one devised to keep dry flies high enough on the water to be seen as clearly by the fisherman as by the trout—hence the name "bivisible."

To put it simply, bivisibles are tied like my streamside offerings described above. Two or more hackle feathers are wrapped tightly around a bare hook. A body is not needed: It would add unnecessary weight and would be obliterated, anyway, by the mass of fluted hackle fibers surrounding the hook shaft in a circle. This complete coverage of a lightweight dry-fly hook shaft with stiff hackle fibers results in the optimum in floatability. Also, individual fibers dry quickly during casting. So a well-tied bivisible of quality hackle literally bounces, even on the roughest water.

In order to render these flies more visible to the fisherman, Mr. Hewitt tied in a white hackle feather in front of the fly. This contrasted clearly with the rest of it, usually brown, since he believed that dark surface flies could be seen by trout more clearly than those of lighter colors. Size, he stressed, is more important than color and overall appearance, so the imitation of wings and tails did not seem important to him.

Many tyers do put tail fibers into bivisibles, for they lend an additional assist to a fly's floatability. Tail or none, the bivisible is a perfect first tie for the novice. All he needs is a hook, some thread, two or three straight hackle fibers (the tail), and two or three neck feathers of any color or size.

Even on slow-moving limestone streams—as well as on the smoother-surfaced freestone waters—there are times when bivisibles can work wonders. During early morning and evening, rising trout can't be so selective as to an insect's anatomical conformation. As long as its size approaches that of the naturals they're after, a bivisible will often produce as well as the most carefully tied direct imitation. Also, when slow-water trout are working on surface midges—the tiniest of flies—bivisible midge imitations can be deadly.

That word "surface" is important. Sometimes trout feed on small terrestrial insects such as jassids. These beetlelike bugs float in the surface film. The common rise for them is a quiet bulging of the surface. Since terrestrials are out of their element in water, trout can take their time. But when aquatic midges are fluttering on the surface and over it—like their larger May fly cousins—trout must be quick to nail them or they'll fly off. So the rise form for surface midges is often fast and splashy. Sometimes trout will clear water and nail them on the wing. Tiny bivisibles on No. 18 or 20 hooks are the answer. Their minuscule size precludes need for direct anatomical imitation. Even on the slickest surfaces trout can't easily distinguish them from phonies.

There's another factor in making any size of bivisible effective. Some maintain that sunlight reflected off a bundle of hackle fibers, bouncing on riffled water, gives trout the impression of an insect's beating wings—a powerful come-on to surface feeders anywhere.

Mr. Hewitt believed that there were three phases in a fly fisherman's development. In the beginning he wants to take as many fish as possible; then he tries for the big ones; in the end, his goal is to fool the wisest fish. Mr. Hewitt's own brainchild, the bivisible, makes each stage of the maturing fly fisherman's development easier to come by.

The almost exclusive fishing of my home-tied bivisibles for three or four years prior to the experience with Dick Sherbahn enabled me to kick the dry-fly mesmerism syndrome. I loved to tie them. Their construction was so uncomplicated that it seemed impossible to tie a bad one.

I'll never forget a winter evening in the late 1950s when I was tying bivisibles and ruminating about G. E. M. Skue's book *The Way of a Trout with a Fly,* which I had just finished.

In questioning his friend Halford's belief in exacting insect imitation, Skue proposed that it is enough for fly anglers to *represent* to the trout facimiles of his natural food since it is, after all, impossible to duplicate naturals perfectly. Thus, the best that an angler can possibly do is to represent or suggest rather than imitate. Of course any artificial is in a general sense an imitation. But to me, at that time an aspiring tying hatch-matcher, discovery of impressionistic theory in the fishing of artificials was of great moment. I was as pleased as punch to realize that beyond proving to myself that I could tie presentable, floatable and workable dry flies, I *had* in a real sense "represented" natural flies to the trout. I had not, of course, hatch-matched with my bivisibles in a strict sense. But in recalling the fact that bivisibles can roughly represent (or

71

suggest) stone and caddis flies—and, in their smaller sizes, midges—I reveled in the dawning realization that I had matched trout's natural surface food, albeit only in a general way.

No longer awed by the mystique surrounding in-depth hatch-matching, I went back to tying tried-and-true patterns and was thrilled to find them taking fish with a fair degree of consistency. I was no longer upset when some failed to float as well as they might have. Rather, I was stimulated to strive for better ties come next winter. Impressionistic theory caused me to develop a dry-fly stratagem that I subsequently dubbed "seasonal hatch-matching" in an *Outdoor Life* article. Simply put, I strove to develop cross-section representations of May flies predominating in early, mid and late season. Most major early-season hatches are of blue-gray coloration. During mid-season browns are common, as are whites and pale yellows in late summer.

During a winter of long firelit evenings I labored over the vise with every imaginable book on fly patterns piled high about me. The final result was a line of variant dry flies, each of which represented in color and size the main features of a given season's principal patterns. Of course, there is no method of determining the efficacy of trout flies with acid-test finality. But I soon convinced myself that these flies were effective. The dressings are as follows:

Gray Variant: early season. Hook: 12 or 14. Body: gray fur or wool, ribbed with peacock quill. Hackle: blue dun mixed with black tail. Dun barbs.

Brown Variant: midseason. Hook: 10. Body: brown fur or wool wound with peacock quill. Hackle: mixed ginger and grizzly. Tail: cock pheasant fibers. Tying thread: olive silk.

Cream Variant (Art Flick): late season. Hook: 12. Body: light cock quill. Hackle: cream color. Tail: cream cock barbs. Tying thread: primrose silk.

Later I realized that central to the seasonal variants' success was the fact that they were fished with confidence. If, for example, I fished one of these flies when nothing like it was on the water I could be reasonably certain that something quite like it should be, just had been, or soon would be emerging. Outdoor columnist Owen Haines had written in the *Lancaster Sunday News* that use of these variant dries eased his transition from a tyro to a serious hatch-matcher. Once he realized that he had matched seasonal representations of fly life, the next step toward more specific representation (or imitating) could be taken without the fears and trepidations common to many an aspiring dry-fly tyer and practioner.

As I see it now, my own transition to more sophisticated insect matching was slower in coming for two very good reasons. First, there were very few occasions when I couldn't catch rising trout (on freestone streams) without having to resort to letter-perfect dry renditions of the hatch or hatches in evidence. Usually, rough suggestions, in color and size, sufficed. Sometimes veritable oddballs worked wonders, such as a fan or hair wing Royal Coachman when a distinctive hatch of naturals was being taken. The effect was to reinforce my strong predeliction toward impressionism. I still harbored misgivings about my ability to recognize and identify fly life. Besides, cheesecloth insect nets and vials of formaldehyde seemed bothersome, and they reminded me of prep-school biology, which I had hated.

Sometimes while tying I became dissatisfied with my work and told myself—almost out loud—that it was high time that I repaired with really serious intent to fly pattern books and attempt the real toughies, challenging ties that looked as if they were about to hatch from the vise. Then I'd go back to the vise, but not to those biologically perfect specimens in the books. Art Flick's patterns were easier to handle. Some other evening I really would get down to tying seriously—some night when I had all the right components and when I'd absolutely *refuse* to allow complicated thoraxes and segmented wrappings in sourcebooks to remind me of those biology tomes of unhappy memory!

Almost imperceptibly, however, I began to become a bit more energetic in my fly tying. Realization that there were definite times and places for exacting imitations and that I'd very likely missed out—without realizing it—at said times and places began to dawn. One particular chain of events in the Poconos during July 1969 was dramatically instructive.

My fishing diary reports that on July 1, 1969, at 8:30 P.M. (the first day of our vacation) my attention was riveted on a handsome 15-inch brown trout lazily devouring nymphs. He was on graveled shallows about 20 feet upstream from my casting position in the tail of a long, satin-smooth pool. My Light Cahill dry fly had been repeatedly refused. I replaced it with a nymph version. He turned that down too. With periodic undulating flashes of his gold-brown flanks, the trout moved forward to deeper water.

As his contours faded, the intensity of the body flashes increased. They had a hypnotizing effect. Momentarily, I was distracted by a larger flash. I guessed that the fish had shifted broadside to me so that his entire length was caught instantaneously in the blood-red sunset behind me. But when his belly blazed again, it was obvious that I was wrong. For, concurrently, a much longer sheen flared brightly a couple of feet beyond the first. It was as if subterranean elves were signaling with a huge, gold-tinted mirror that spelled *big trout!* Abruptly, I came to my senses. Two fish were nymphing, the 15-incher and another, much larger, maybe 20 inches.

As big brown trout go, the latter was no record-breaker. But a fish's size is relative to its habitat. This stream was small, 20 feet across at its widest. In the '68 season the largest trout taken was a 22-inch brown. At this time the '69 record stood at 18 inches—another brown trout. By anyone's yardstick the second trout was a trophy fish, and the first would come close to the '69 record. Landing either would be exciting.

Happily, I had the rest of July to try. Since trout often come slowly during the daylight hours of the dog days, I decided to try for these two lunkers after sundown when fly activity increased and fish fed more actively.

The next day at 7:45 P.M. fish were surface-feeding with a vengeance on Yellow Sally stone flies. I tried to match the hatch with a No. 14 Cream Variant dry fly. Action was wild. Eight legal-size trout were caught and released by 8:15, when I rounded the last bend and faced the pool, now flushed orange-red in the sun's afterglow. In its tail small trout were rising. Midway up the right bank and hard against it a nice fish (I guessed it was the 15-incher) was gulping flies—but only flies that floated under overhanging grass and into his mouth. It was a tough float to duplicate. Several casts put my fly too far from the bank, and the trout refused to budge for it.

A cast to the right of a small waterfall at the pool's head brought the desired float. As it began, a huge shadowy dorsal fin protruded slowly. Breathless, I stood rooted to the gravel as the largest trophy trout sank, and my fly meandered on. It was in the line of drift that I'd wanted originally. This time the 15-incher surfaced, slowly and deliberately, like his big brother at the head of the pool. But he also refused.

At 8:45 a small hatch of little Sulphurs emerged, and the tempo of rising increased. A No. 18 Light Cahill seemed a good imitation. After fitting my tying light with its magnifying glass, I easily attached the small fly to a fine 6X leader tippet. I cast to the falls and rose the biggest trout, but he refused again. As the fly neared the lie of the second fish, it brushed against a drooping blade of grass and swung into a slow half-turn against the bank. Ever so slowly the trout moved forward and drank it in.

I set the hook, and he bolted toward the falls. In its white water the trim, tawny brownie broke clear in an arching high jump. He sounded deep and began circular runs. After four or

75

five minutes of wearing him down, I finally netted him. He was highly colored and measured 15 3/4 inches. Since this sophisticated stream-bred fish was taken by successful hatch-matching, I was convinced that his larger mate could be tempted the same way—at sunset when his sharp perception would be impaired by fading light.

For the rest of that week I failed to raise the big fish on imitation of the one fly that was consistently on the water: Yellow Sally. On July 9 a sparse hatch of Pale Evening Dun May flies interested him. After watching him sip a couple of naturals I conned a rise with my counterfeit. But no take.

I finally hooked the big fellow on July 15 at 8:50 P.M. Heavy rains had fallen during the preceding weekend. Since terrestrial insects are often washed into streams by rains, I decided on a No. 14 Ant. *It was murder.* I wrote in my fishing diary:

> Took seven nice fish below the pool in 15 minutes. Hit pool at 8:30. Had trouble seeing Ant by this time. But was able to get a proper drift against the bank by letting the current take over from the falls. On the first cast my Ant floated smack into the kisser of my granddaddy brown. . . .

The nonchalant take proved that he was perfectly duped. When I set the hook he was stirred into a head-long reel-stripping rush for the white water. There he dug deep and circled with the slow, majestic precision of a merry-go-round. After four revolutions he settled in deep water. I prodded him into a fifth go-around. Now he moved up—a few inches below the surface. Instinctively, I moved into the pool and got a good look at 20 inches of prime, bespeckled brown trout. But he must have detected my movement. For he rocketed toward the bank, and the leader flew free.

Cursing the stupidity of my move, I groped on shaking legs to a boulder and collapsed on it. Thanks to the soothing effects of gurgling water in gathering darkness, I soon regained my composure.

Darkness! I suddenly realized that I'd been night fishing, and previously I'd sought this trout by twilight. My fine 6X leader tippet was unnecessary. The trout could never have noticed a heavier one—say, 3X—so chances of a break-off would have been nil. By the same token, imitating specific flies was unnecessary.

I should have realized from experience that big trout often kick their inhibitions at night. Since predators are robbed by darkness of good visiblity and easy pickings, trout freely cruise from daytime lairs in quest of varying foods: minnows, large nocturnal flies such as moths, grasshoppers, crickets, even frogs and mice.

My mistake was not hatch-matching at twilight. That was the only possible way to con strikes from that wise old brown by day. But after dark, heavier tackle and larger nocturnal imitations might have been more productive.

I had been fishing with a six-foot, two-ounce bamboo fly rod. Its light weight facilitated fishing those small flies on a fine leader. The action of heavier rods sometimes snaps 5X and 6X tippets. But imitations of large food forms are wind-resistant and difficult to cast on small rods. An eight-footer with heavier line and leader was the answer.

Unfortunately, nasty weather and the diverting commitments that plague anglers on family vacations previously kept me from the stream. On the 16th I had my first opportunity. At 9:30 P.M. I began with No. 4 deer-hair bass flies. One hour of fishing yielded four small browns, and the large trout never rose.

The low-pressure area that had plagued the Poconos continued. Vainly, I waited for clearing weather. Since vacation time was fast running out, I disregarded dripping skies, went back to the stream at 10:00 P.M. on July 22, and decided to play dirty. From my bass tackle box I dug up a large deer-hair frog. I cast it to the foot of the falls. It barely began its drift before erupting water crashed loudly. Line hissed through the guides as my trophy trout plunged deep. When he hugged bottom I prodded him sharply. There was little need to fear for the 2X leader.

The big fish rose slowly and began to circle at pool center. After a dozen minutes of wearing him down, I had him on his side. I guided him back to the shallows and beached him. He measured an even 20 inches.

Hatch-matching dry-fly purists might feel like drumming me out of the corps, for it seemed downright unsporting to take advantage of that lusty and wise old trout under cover of darkness when he was unselective and eager for a mouthful. And on a bass lure, to boot! Perhaps I would have never stooped to conquer if my vacation had not been almost over.

This year's month-long vacation in the Poconos is now over; we drive home tomorrow. I've just written the last entry in my diary:

> One and one half hours fished, weather temp. 80; barometer up; sunny; water temp. 60; clear, low. Fly species: Yellow Sally. Notes: Last Outing of our most enjoyable of vacations. Fished from golf course to M. Falls. Fish on Yellow Sallys all the way. I fished Royal Wulff and they wouldn't touch it! Very selective! Fished R. Wulff in big pool at falls to no avail. Rested for twenty minutes there; then went to Yellow Sally imitations (a pretty good one) and took fish. Five before dark. All released. A pure and simple hatch-matching situation.

Quite by chance I finished this evening on the same pool in which I worked over that large brownie in '69. And by chance, too, these fish were as selective as their old granddaddy. For, as noted, I came upon them with a Royal Wulff, and they didn't want it any more than their brethren downstream. Tonight it just had to be the Yellow Sally, and I'm convinced that they were effective because they were good imitations—the results of my more purposeful tying over recent winters. So

I could not quell a surge of pride while relaxing by the pool as bats began picking off airborne Sallys amidst falling shadows.

As I gazed on the darkening pool, broken only occasionally now by rising fish, the glow of well-being persisted, prompted by recollections of a short piece I'd written about this, my favorite stream, a few years back in The Angler's Club *Bulletin* (The Angler's Club of New York). It was called "A Last Day," and I'll repeat it here:

All of us who fish for trout harbor fond recollections of "Opening," or "First Days." Time may blur the dates of specific openings, but never experiences to which they gave rise, be said experiences exciting, frustrating, funny or whimsical. Few of us, though, are possessed of clear memories of the "last days" of our years astream. Unless a given season's outing was dominated by a standout happening, recollections of it fly—as the old hymn goes—"Forgotten as a dream dies at the waking day."

As of October 10, 1970, I became as aware of "last days" as "first days," thanks to an experience rendered memorably whimsical by an impending tragedy.

Earlier in the year my favorite trout stream was sentenced to death by the U.S. Soil Conservation Service. It's a club stream in Pennsylvania's Pocono Mountains, stocked in the lower reaches but occupied by a fine head of stream-bred brown trout (and some native brookies) throughout most of its length. The floods of 1955 and 1969 provided the S.C.S. its rationale. A dam would protect the village at the stream's mouth. Protestations by club members were to no avail.

So I planned what seemed a last outing on the stream at the time of a weekend convention my wife and I were to attend in the Poconos. Sally dropped me off at the stream's lower stretch early on Saturday afternoon. At 5:30 P.M. she was to pick me up at the top, a distance of three and a half miles.

The day was virtually cloudless and very bright, with a titillating nip of autumn. Mountain leafage presented a breathtaking tableau of vivid reds and yellows. There was a sparse hatch of

Cahill-like flies coming off the water. Trout were as eager to take my artificial as they were to gobble naturals, and they were inordinately eager. I took fish almost at will—more, I think, than I'd ever taken on the stream in 21 years of fishing it. There were many high-jumping browns, plump and beautifully attired in bright spawning colors.

I saw several deer. And on rounding a tall telephone-booth-shaped boulder, I saw a red fox scamper from the shadows into a sunlit clearing. He stopped abruptly, threw me a quick, quizzical look and was off. I was amazed at how much his face resembled that of an acquaintance. I collapsed on a rock and laughed, loud and long. Then I met the porcupine.

He was crouched about 20 feet away, staring at me. He moved toward a thin sapling and tried to climb it. It bent under his weight, and he fell on his behind. Ashamed, he looked at me with his head lowered. Then he chanced another climb and fell. Again he looked shamefacedly in my direction. After a third fall he waddled into the woods, now echoing with my laughter.

About 4:00 P.M. swarms of May flies—Isonychia Bicolors, I believe—began mating dances overhead. Later, when spinners began to touch water, trout fed wildly. They took all artificials offered, and I experimented with at least a half-dozen patterns.

At 5:00 P.M. I reached the bridge over the stream where Sally was to pick me up. Sitting on a rock in midstream, I dressed out a nice brace of browns for our Sunday breakfast. When I was done I remained sitting, watching May flies and the feeding trout. My booted right foot was hanging a couple of inches above the surface of a shallow glide. Directly underneath I noticed a brook trout, a scant six inches long. He must have thought my boot an overhanging rock. For after moving out to snatch a spinner, he returned and took up the same position. The feeding procedure was followed four times.

Then—just for the hell of it—I very slowly reached for my leader, on which was attached a Red Quill, and flicked it to the surface above my boot. As it reached it, the brookie moved out and struck viciously but either missed or spit out the fly. Back under my boot he went.

I lay the leader on the rock and watched him, just below the boot. Three spinners drifted by, and he didn't budge. Finally, he kicked his recently instilled misgivings and took a fourth.

A horn tooted. Sally had parked the wagon on the bridge. Somehow I could not leave the little trout. I hadn't thought about the dam all day. Then it came to mind. "A little fellow like this," I mused, "won't stand the silt when construction begins."

Sally was leaning over the bridge imploring me to get a move on. As I hoisted the boot the little trout darted away. I felt a hot tear blocking my right eyelid and very audibly said "goodbye"—to the brookie, the gossamer-winged May flies hovering over Wild Cat Hollow, the stream. The stream's sentence was commuted by federal budget cuts. Now the job, we are given to understand, "will be done in '75." So I'll have yet another "last day" there. But it can't be as memorable as the first.

I could have joyfully written a postscript to this story in the winter of 1975. The dam was stopped, maybe even for keeps. Some dedicated local residents successfully took the S.C.S. into federal court and got me to testify in Williamsport on behalf of the fly-angling fraternity. To few of us is it given to help save our favorite waters from the federal bulldozer. Hence the prideful glow I felt at streamside this evening.

My favorite stream, I mused on beginning the trek back to the cottage. Why? Certainly I'd fished wilder waters for larger trout, even pastoral streams for more sophisticated browns. Nor did my affection for this particular segment of the Brodheads watershed stem entirely from a long and intimate association. Such relationships—like that which inures with a good wife—are sometimes the better for teaching one something. This, I guessed, was the source of my abiding affection for the little stream. As my veritable hothouse for experimentation with fly patterns it served to stimulate my interest in fly tying, thus enabling me to savor the pleasures of two-dimensional fly angling.

Tomorrow I shall return to August's humid days in the

office, pleasantly punctuated by occasional evenings on the Letort with Charlie Fox. All too soon the plaintive chirps of cicadas will signal the end of a fallow summer and the children's return to school. Then autumnal hues brightly smearing the southern ridge near my home will remind me to examine fly-tying materials. All must be in order for the first snowfall, my traditional time to begin a new angling year—at the card table.

DRY FLIES

The fly tyer who has spent considerable time learning the fundamentals by tying enough of the previously described flies should have no trouble with the dry fly. I might add that the mark of a good fly tyer is judged by the quality and neatness of the dry fly he ties.

We will start with a simple hackle dry fly but will use peacock eye quill for the body.

Before starting on this fly, let's assemble all of the material we will need to complete the fly. I would suggest from now on, when you are going to tie a certain pattern, that you have all the material laid out and ready to use for the number of flies you are going to tie.

First, select good stiff-fibered throat or spade hackle for tail material, then two of the best-quality neck hackle. Strip off the soft downy part of the stump end. This is usually the bottom third. Remember that the fibers should be one and one half to two times as long as the gap of the hook. Take quill from the peacock eye and remove the fine, hairlike fuzz from the quill. This can be done by using a soft eraser and lightly stroking from the tip to the butt end.

We are now ready to start tying the fly.

Tie on eight or ten good stiff fibers for the tail (same as wet fly). Now tie in the quill by the butt end so that the dark side faces the rear of the fly (Diagram #1). Wind tying thread toward the eye of the hook, building up any irregularities until the base is smooth. This will make it easier to wind on the quill. Stop one-third distance back of eye. Now wind on quill and tie off one-third distance back of eye.

Place the two selected hackles so the dull sides face out and tie in close to the body by the stump end. Some tyers lay the hackle so that the top sides are together, but I personally like to tie in my hackle as just described because I do not like the hackle to fan out. After the hackles are secured, wind tying thread up toward eye, but be sure to leave enough room to tie off the hackles (Diagram #2). Grasp tip of front hackle and start winding toward eye of hook. Be sure to keep each turn as close to the preceding one as possible. Always keep the dull side facing the eye. Wind up to point illustrated in Diagram #3 and tie off. One or two turns of second hackle should be made close

KEEP BODY
SMOOTH

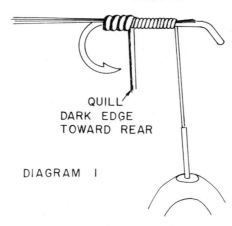

QUILL
DARK EDGE
TOWARD REAR

DIAGRAM 1

AFTER STUMP ENDS
ARE SECURE — CUT
OFF EXCESS

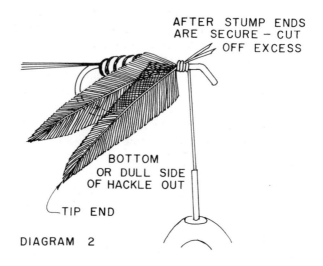

BOTTOM
OR DULL SIDE
OF HACKLE OUT

TIP END

DIAGRAM 2

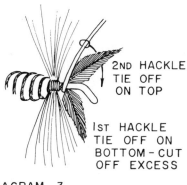

2ND HACKLE
TIE OFF
ON TOP

IST HACKLE
TIE OFF ON
BOTTOM - CUT
OFF EXCESS

DIAGRAM 3

against rear of first hackle. When you reach the front of the first hackle, hold the first hackle fibers back and make one or two turns around in the front but not tight enough to bend the fibers back. Now tie off and complete fly with half hitches or whip finish.

Palmer Fly

The Palmer fly is nothing more than a hackle ribbed body fly (Diagram #4 should sufficiently illustrate this step). Tie in material in the following order: tail, ribbing hackle, body material. Wind on body, then rib with hackle. Now tie in two hackle at front and finish off the same as with the hackle dry fly.

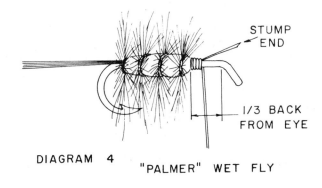

STUMP
END

1/3 BACK
FROM EYE

DIAGRAM 4   "PALMER" WET FLY

85

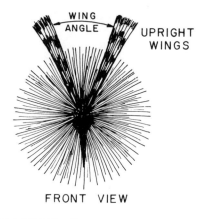

FRONT VIEW

DIAGRAM 5

Winged Dry Flies

We will only describe and illustrate the method for the two most popular types of wings for the dry fly. Before tying any wings, study Diagram #5. This is the correct wing position for the upright winged dry fly.

Diagram #6 illustrates the two most common methods of preparing breast or flank feathers for the divided wing. Select a feather that is well marked and of uniform quality. Strip off all downy and uneven fibers from stump end until feathers simulate diagram. If the feather is large enough for the size fly you are tying, a section from one side may be large enough to make the wings. If not, then cut a section from each side, as in (A). When feather is small, cut out center, as in (B). The length of wing determines how far back to cut out center.

Attach tying thread to hook and wind up to one-third distance back of eye. If section or sections cut from side of feathers are used, be sure ends are even. Hold in compact bunch and tie in (Diagram #7). Remember, wings should be one-fourth longer than hackle. Use the same procedure as used when tying in the tail. After wing material is secured, grasp wing material and pull up, as in Diagram #8. Wind tying thread in front so that wing material will stand erect. Use both hands

PULL
ENDS
TOGETHER
AND TIE IN
ONE BUNCH

Ⓐ   Ⓑ

DIAGRAM 6

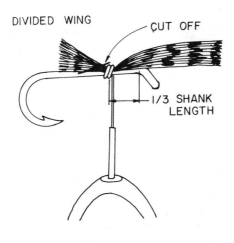

DIVIDED WING   CUT OFF

1/3 SHANK
LENGTH

DIAGRAM 7

87

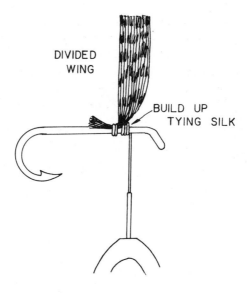

DIAGRAM 8

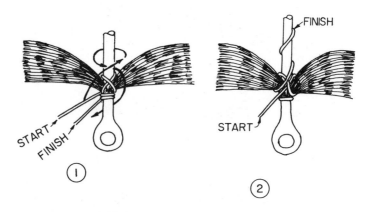

DIAGRAM 9

and separate fibers into two even bunches, then follow Diagram #9 to cock wings. Next spiral tying thread back on shank, tie in tail, then wind on body and tie two dry fly hackle back of wing. Wind first hackle back of wings and tie off in front of wings. Take one or two turns of second hackle back of first hackle (described in hackle dry fly), spiral up and save enough to make three or four turns close to wings in front. Tie off and secure by appropriate hitches.

Hair and spent wings are tied on in exactly the same way. The hair wing procedure is the same as for divided wings. Hackle tips are used for spent wings. Crisscross tying thread between wings until wings are in spent position.

Quill Section Wings

Quill section wings are the most difficult for the beginner. However, if you have practiced enough with the quill section winged wet fly, you should have no trouble.

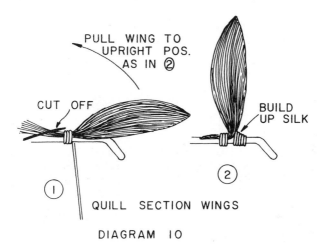

QUILL SECTION WINGS

DIAGRAM 10

Diagram #10 shows the procedure for setting the wings. After securing tying thread, wind it up to one-third distance back of eye. Strip off bottom section of matched quills until the fibers are uniform. Cut a section from each quill. Check Diagrams #9 and 10 (wet fly section). Be sure not to cut wing too wide. It is best for the beginner to have the wings no wider than the gap of the hook. Lay wings together so convex sides are against each other. Hold so wing tips are out over eye and so they will be about a fourth longer than the fibers of the

89

hackle. Secure by the same method as used for the wet fly. Grasp wings securely between thumb and finger of left hand and pull upright, make enough turns of tying silk in front of wings to hold them erect. To separate wings, make a loose crisscross between wings (Diagram #9). Before tightening up thread, grasp wings at base and squeeze gently, tighten up thread at this time. If you neglect to do this, the wing will twist and split. All other steps are the same as for the divided wing dry fly.

SUGGESTED DRY FLY PATTERNS

Name	Head	Tail	Ribbing	Body	Hackle	Wing
Adams	black	mixed barred Plymouth Rock and brown hackle barbules		gray fur or wool	mixed barred Plymouth Rock and brown	barred Plymouth Rock hackle points
Sulphur (Harvey)	yellow	light ginger hackle barbules		rabbit fur yellow orange, pink and white mixed	light ginger and light orange	white hackle tips
Quill Gordon	black	rusty blue dun or blue dun hackle barbules		stripped peacock eye quill	blue dun or rusty blue dun	wood duck
Light Cahill	cream	light ginger hackle barbules		light cream	light ginger	wood duck
Black Gnat	black	black hackle barbules		black fur or wool	black	gray mallard quill

90

4. "Limestone Streams Have Made the Art of Diminution the Tying Angler's Ultimate Challenge"

—CHARLES K. FOX

SINCE 1496, when Dame Juliana Berners popularized it as a pastime, fly fishing has evolved through five distinct phases. Wet flies held center stage until the late nineteenth century, when metallurgical advances enabled England's George Selwyn Marryat and Frederick Halford to develop dry flies. Another Englishman, G. E. M. Skues, introduced nymph imitations in the early twentieth century. Then followed Theodore Gordon's American wet fly innovation, the streamer. In the 1950s the American team of Vincent C. Marinaro and Charles K. Fox introduced terrestrial insect imitations. This breakthrough is generally accepted as the most significant of all, because it enabled fly anglers and tyers to achieve the optimum in the art of deception.

For hundreds of years the principal insect imitated by trout fishermen was the aquatic May fly. It never occurred to fly fishermen on both sides of the Atlantic that under certain conditions trout will feed heavily on a wide variety of terrestrial insects. The food-rich "chalk" streams of England are like limestone streams in the United States in that they flow through limestone-based soil that is highly productive of zoo

91

plankton, the microscopic basis of nature's "food chain," and supportive of great quantities of aquatic and terrestrial insect life.

Ernest Schwiebert in his charming book *Remembrances of Rivers Past* (Macmillan) graphically describes Vince Marinaro's discovery on Letort Spring Run in south-central Pennsylvania during the mid 1950s:

> He stopped fishing to study the current. Prone in the warm grass, Marinaro watched the slow current pattern slide hypnotically past. Some time elapsed in pleasant reverie before he was suddenly aware of minute insects on the water. He rubbed his eyes but they were really there; minuscule Mayflies struggling with their diaphanous nymphal skins, tiny beetles like minute bubbles, ants awash in the surface film, and countless minutiae pinioned in the smooth current.
>
> His mind stirred with excitement as he hurried toward the fishing hut. There he quickly fashioned a fine mesh seine with sticks and mosquito netting. His meshes were not long in the water before his suspicions were confirmed by the thin residue of tiny insects collected at the water line. There were Mayflies with wings less than an eighth-inch in length, beetles less than 3/32nds of an inch in diameter, tiny reddish, gold and black ants an eighth-inch in length, and leaf hoppers of minute dimension in astonishing numbers.

The full story of Vince and Charlie's development of terrestrial insect imitations has been oft repeated in the burgeoning literature of limestone angling that commenced during the late 1950s and early 1960s. The seminal works are Vince Marinaro's *A Modern Dry Fly Code* (Crown) and Charlie Fox's *This Wonderful World of Trout* and *Rising Trout* (Freshet)—"must" reading for one who would fish limestone waters.

America's prime Eastern limestone trout streams are mostly located in central and south-central Pennsylvania. The larger streams in the Allegheny Mountains such as Spring Creek, Penn's Creek, and Spruce Creek have been meccas for trout fishermen for many years. The smaller south-central streams, not so well known until the Marinaro–Fox terrestrial breakthrough, are Falling Springs, Letort Spring Run, Green Spring Creek, Big Spring, Boiling Springs, and the Yellow Breeches, the latter being the largest of this region's trout streams. These waters have the characteristics of England's chalk rivers. Amid undulating pastoral country they meander slowly, their placid waters cooled by strong underground springs.

The volume of both aquatic and terrestrial fish food is tremendous: fry fish, minnows, May flies, caddis flies, and stone flies, together with a variety of beetles, bugs, ants, crickets, and grasshoppers. This rich insect food supply is replaced during the winter months by an immense amount of sow (cress) bugs and freshwater shrimp. As a result, limestone trout are extraordinarily well conditioned and quickly reach large proportions.

From the time of the first pioneers trout have been taken from these lovely streams by all manner of rigs. Theodore Gordon, the patron saint of American fly angling, fished them with flies, as in later years did many others. Few, however, tried to match natural insect hatches and thus experience the pleasure of stalking rising trout in the British way. Fewer, if any, realized that terrestrial insects represent a substantial amount of the food for limestone trout. If some observant souls did take note of the fact, they made no known effort to imitate terrestrials before Fox and Marinaro.

Fast-flowing freestone water serves to disguise sloppy fly presentation. But the generally smooth, even-flowing limestone streams throughout central Pennsylvania, like their fabled English equivalents, permit few mistakes. Limestone neophytes invariably discover this on their first outings. Many give up the ghost on the spot. I almost did.

I was visiting Charlie and Glad Fox about fifteen years ago at their home on the banks of the Letort. Japanese beetles were very much in season that beautiful summer day, and a smart breeze was consistantly blowing them into the stream. My first shock came when I saw the size of some of the trout that were lazily devouring the beetles. It seemed impossible that such big fish could inhabit so small a stream—and in such great numbers! The second shock came when Charlie attached to my line over 10 feet of leader, tapered to the unheard of (to me) size of 7X! Shock number three bade fair to steal my breath away when about 20 feet above us a pair of immense brown trout rose slowly and menacingly—for all the world like two U-boats in a wolf pack—until their uptilted snouts bulged above the surface. Each drank in a beetle and settled back into the depths.

Charlie silently singled out the largest for me to tempt with one of his split coffee bean Japanese beetle imitations. I insisted that he first try his hand for my edification. Like a stalking Indian he crept noiselessly up the left bank. The fish lay in a channel bordered by a bed of watercress against the right bank and a parallel strip of elodea in center stream. After measuring the distance with a couple of false casts, Charlie dropped his beetle at two o'clock, about 15 feet ahead of the trout's lie. It floated smack into the "take" zone. I almost heard my heart beat as the big brown began his slow rise. For a second he looked over the lure. Then, perfectly conned, he sipped it in. As Charlie struck, the brownie, as if momentarily electrified, sped up stream and the screeching reel drowned out the dreamy chirp of cicadas.

Charlie fought the fish for several minutes. But it got too firmly embedded in elodea and broke off. While he landed two smaller trout before a tangerine sun sank behind the Allegheny foothills, it was obvious that Charlie's real pleasure lay in duping the trout rather than landing them. In order to do this, his presentation had to be letter perfect. Were the drift off target, had the beetle alighted too close to the fish, or if the leader were delivered in a bunched or coiled state, these trout

94

would never have been duped. It was plain to see that this kind of fishing demanded a high degree of skill. Perhaps a dawning inferiority complex was responsible for my bad showing. With very little effort I managed to make each of the above-mentioned *faux pas* (bad floats, "close in" casts, sloppy leader delivery), and I paid the price. Not one trout I fished over was hooked.

Had I been typical of some dedicated freestone anglers, one such limestone outing would have been enough. I would have foregone this potentially exciting angling—not to mention tying the interesting new patterns to which it gave rise—for more familiar mountain streams whose gurgling rapids and singing glides are so thankfully forgiving of mistakes! Fortunately, I was not so dedicated a "mountainman" as to give up on these wary, pasture-land fish. They were close to home. There was plenty of time to practice over them whenever I got the urge. And, of course, the pleasing, Old World charm of limestone waters was hypnotic. So I went back. Over the years I have learned to cope well enough to fool these fish occasionally, which, as I learned that first afternoon, constitutes a more important challenge than landing them. Thankfully, these experiences have opened vistas for me as a fly tyer.

It's a pity that terrestrial insects and limestone waters have come to have a bacon-and-eggs relationship. While the many writings on limestone trout fishing cover aquatics—particularly small May flies—the magnitude of the terrestrial discovery was sufficient to prompt authors to stress terrestrials; hence the popular tendency to equate them almost exclusively with limestone waters. The majority of these imitations are minute, as tough to tie as they are to fish. So from its inception limestone angling was widely deemed a pursuit fit only for expert anglers and tyers. Many fledgling and sometime anglers fail to realize that certain easy-to-tie terrestrials can be simply and effectively fished on freestone streams and, conversely, that their customary aquatic patterns can often be fished just as effectively and easily on limestone streams.

For example, limestone streams in north-central Pennsylvania have some large May fly hatches, such as the legendary Green Drake Hatch on Penn's Creek, not to mention those on Spruce and Spring creeks. On these rivers also, from early season to mid-July, there are ample to large hatches of the Sulphur, Blue Quill, Little Olive, and Caenis. An angler visiting these particular waters—after checking with native regulars who are always easy to find—can quickly learn what imitations to have in his fly box. And if flies aren't coming off the water at a given time, he will know what should be in the process of hatching. So he can use nymph imitations. This is exactly the procedure he would follow on a freestone stream.

In the south-central Pennsylvania limestone watershed May fly hatches are not so heavy or so varied, although there is an excellent early-season hatch of Hendrickson's on the Yellow Breeches. The Sulphur and Little Olive are also important flies, as is the Caenis on Falling Springs. All of these flies are easy ties for any fly tyer.

While terrestrial insects are important trout fare in the north-central region (especially later in the season) they're a bigger factor to the south, thanks to the relative sparseness of May flies there. Since minute terrestrial imitations require such great care in presentation, a beginning limestone fly fisherman would do well to sample north-central streams in Pennsylvania before taking on those in the south. For the northern streams more resemble freestone waters, and there is better opportunity there to fish the more familiar May fly imitations.

Streamers can be very effective on larger and more riffled limestone streams, and streamerettes are often deadly on the smaller, more placid waters such as the Letort, particularly in early season when fly hatches are scant. On all limestone streams slow and deeply fished nymphs can be very productive, especially when they are close imitations of the naturals present at the time.

Fly-tying anglers, then, can approach limestone streams with their favorite aquatic imitations and be successful. But once they gain confidence in their ability to fish these placid waters, they should attempt terrestrial imitations, if for no other reason than that terrestrials represent such an important factor in the diet of trout in all limestone streams. Contrary to popular belief, many terrestrial imitations are easy to tie.

On a hot midsummer afternoon about 20 years ago I was fishing the Catskill's Schoharie hard but to no avail. The few fish that rose would take none of a wide range of dry flies. Nymphs and streamerettes evoked nary a bump. When I was about to call it quits a rising trout, then another and in several seconds a few more, startled me. The action took place before a large boulder overhanging a bankside patch of glassy backwater. Since no flies were visible, I guessed the trout to be after infinitesimal midges or dipthra. My smallest dry flies were No. 16 and 18 Sulphurs and Adams. They would not produce.

Much to my surprise casting did not put the trout down. They seemed mesmerized by the tiny morsels on which they were feeding.

I went up the bank and crawled carefully to the boulder's brow. About a dozen fair-sized browns and rainbows lay in the slack shallows. I could not maneuver myself higher, in order to glimpse the water directly under the boulder, without scaring off the fish. But in seconds I had the answer. Winged ants were bobbing and weaving across the surface around the boulder's base. I guessed that they were swarming under it and that the trout were on the lookout for wandering strays.

Quietly I backed off and hurried to my station wagon and the seldom-used cigar-box fly-tying kit. Never having tied an ant of any sort, I came up with the obvious: a bare hook wound with black silk into two humps—one fore and one aft—with a tiny black hackle-spear flared through the wasp-waist middle. Even though I used a No. 18 hook and was highly excited, it was not a difficult tie. After tying up a 10-foot leader, tapered to 6X (the better to cope with that almost dead water), I took a casting position directly below the boulder and carefully delivered to the flat. The ant sat flush in the surface film. I twitched it gently. A rainbow broke clear into a half gainer and took in a splashy re-entry. A plump 14-incher, he punctuated a stiff tussle with a couple of high jumps and tail walks. After I released this fish I doctored my ant and presented it as before. Again it was taken, this time by a small brown. Four or five more trout fell to my winged ant before it unraveled —probably thanks to my lack of head cement.

I look back on this experience as one of my most memorable. It seemed incredible that so many trout could be taken repeatedly from a glassy patch of shallow water. It is true that all fish struck closely to the current to enable me to get them into it quickly so as to minimize the disturbance. And I had presented the ant with great caution. Still, under normal conditions it would have been a once and done situation. But somehow those swarming flying ants goaded the trout into an abnormally uninhibited orgy of feeding. They abandoned inbred wariness to such an extent that I almost believe a 2X leader and line in their "windows" would not have fazed them.

I shall never forget this afternoon for another reason: It taught me to kick my inhibitions about the tying and fishing of terrestrial imitations. While I never again experienced anything like a repeat performance with them, I fished winged ants (unwinged ones, too) in late season with good enough results to inspire me to experiment with grasshoppers. I fished only freestone waters in those days. The ants, of course, being so small, were easier fished on placid stretches. Before long it dawned that I just might as well have been on limestone streams. No longer awed by the prospect, I soon became entranced by the delightful Old World idiom of the Letort.

The tying of tiny terrestrial imitations demands more patience than I could muster during my first years of tying. But I handled the larger renditions easily. Most terrestrial ties require more painstaking efforts than aquatic patterns. So, on those occasions when I was more energetic than usual, I attempted them: ants, assorted beetles, grasshoppers, and crickets. During my "terrestrial sessions" I experienced a greater sense of satisfaction than ever before, because these offerings —more than the others—had to dupe trout in their own right. There was precious little water in the Letort, Big Spring, or Falling Springs capable of disguising their imperfections, so it was incumbent on me (the generally lazy tyer) to "play over my head." When I did, my sense of self-fulfillment peaked, for now I had graduated into the ranks of the pastime's elitists, those "limestoners" who tie their own!

A great boon to limestone anglers has been the opening, by the Pennsylvania Fish Commission on a "fly fish only" basis, of the south-central Pennsylvania limestone streams year round. The immense quantities of freshwater shrimp and sow bugs available to trout during the winter months are devoured voraciously in a manner as singular as it is fascinating.

Sow bugs and shrimp attach themselves to subsurface grass and elodea. Since they seem to prefer taking both on free floats, trout often snuggle into this vegetation and quite literally shake them loose. Charlie Fox calls this phenomenon "rooting."

My first experience with rooting trout occurred late in fall 1975 while spending a day with Charlie on the Letort. Charlie described the phenomenon in his living room, then rigged up a rod for me, and we walked down his lawn to the stream. He pulled up some waterweeds and pointed to a profusion of shrimp and sow bugs. Then he broke out the counterfeits. Tied on No. 22 hooks, they seemed real enough to crawl off Charlie's hand. With the help of a jeweler's loop he attached a shrimp to a 7X tippet. We relaxed on one of his bankside benches and scanned the still, blue-green surface for a rooting trout. Within several minutes, near stream center, the surface bulged. A few seconds later a trout dimpled a foot or two below the rooting area. The bulge marked the fish's rooting position; the dimple signaled his take of a detached sow bug or a shrimp.

Charlie bade me crouch about 20 feet below the fish, slightly to its left, and to begin roll casting to the rooting position. It was necessary to keep low since there was no tree cover in the area. Roll casting insured minimum rod action, thus reducing the possibility of putting down the fish.

By the time I got into position the fish rooted again. This time his tail broke water. We had a good view of him (a 14-inch brown) burrowing in the streaming grass and shaking it with undulating flanks.

"Cast now," hissed Charlie, "while he's busy."

He backed up as my shrimp dropped just above the fish's rooting spot. Before it reached the trout (on his right) he turned lazily to the left, gobbled a natural and moved back to the rooting position.

My timing had been off. Had I cast a couple of seconds earlier the trout would have been closer to the drifting counterfeit.

As the brownie began to root again I dropped the shrimp in the same area. When he backed up this time it moved directly at him. As it passed, he tipped up gently and took a natural. With an oath I backed up and handed the rod to Charlie.

"You find another and try your hand," I said dejectedly. Charlie quickly pushed me back to the casting position, reminding me in excited whispers that I was in a "different ballgame." To wit: When trout don't take a fly after a good showing it's customary on freestone streams to try him on another—and another, until he takes or you put him down.

"These trout want shrimp and sow bugs. But there's a tremendous number of naturals to choose from," Charlie said. "Just keep after him and be careful!"

I tried this fish four more times, to no avail. Then we spotted a 17- or 18-inch lunker brown several feet ahead that had just begun to root. "Good time to try him!" Charlie whispered.

I presented in like manner to the big fellow, but he failed to show interest in my shrimp. In reply to my plaintive stare, Charlie insisted that it wasn't my shrimp—that I should keep on working him.

The big, deep-girthed brownie showed real interest after the next delivery. Very slowly he went into reverse just beneath it. My rod hand was clammy. I breathed hard as his head tipped up. When those large, chalky jaws parted to sip the lure, building tension got the better of me. Simultaneously, I struck too soon and stood up. The fish disappeared in a flash beneath an emerald bank of elodea. Always the gentleman, Charlie was very understanding. "Just a touch of buck fever," he said and laughed.

We were happily surprised to see that the first trout was still rooting in the same spot. I tried him again for a few minutes. He finally took, with slow breath-stealing deliberation. I timed the strike better this time but did not connect solidly.

Literally wrung out, I returned Charlie's rod and asked for a proper demonstration. He was able to oblige, but not immediately. After getting reactions similar to mine from another 14-incher for a good five or six minutes, Charlie scored.

One trout in an hour and a half is usually symptomatic of a slow day. But this particular brief encounter with the wily browns of the Letort was the proverbial exception proving the rule. Charlie had introduced me to an especially challenging sort of feeding situation, resembling those brought on in summer months by selective surface feeding. There was the same need for painstaking, repetitious casting in order to compete with the plethora of naturals. But Charlie reminded me that during winter months a new factor is involved. A trout's body temperature is that of the water. As temperatures drop, his metabolism slows down. Less food is required, so he eats sparingly, more languidly, and hence with more care than in summer months. As winter lures, then, sow bugs and shrimp present fly tyers with the toughest kind of challenge.

According to Charlie Fox, the most effective patterns are tied by Al Troth, a professional fly tyer from Dillon, Montana. Al was a schoolteacher from Montoursville, Pennsylvania, 20 years ago when Charlie first met him on a visit to the Letort.

"I'll always remember that day," Charlie said, "because Al was driving the first camper that I had ever seen. He took me in the thing and showed me pictures of big brownies taken during his summer vacation in Montana, where he fished spring-fed limestone streams. He gave me a No. 18 shrimp that was very good out there. But I never got around to fishing it —believe it or not—until three years ago when the Letort was opened year round."

Charlie went on to describe how his study of Letort trout's winter feeding habits prompted his trying the fly. "It was murder," he said.

Al Troth had since retired, moved to Montana, and set up as a commercial fly tyer. Charlie wrote for more shrimp and described the sow bugs with which Al was familiar. Charlie received imitations along with the shrimp, and they were just as effective.

Any experienced fly angler is familiar with imitations of these two artificials. They have been around for years, particularly the shrimp, which is sometimes rendered by manufacturers in plastic. But there was one very important difference between most shrimp and sow bug imitations and Al Troth's: Most are tied on No. 14 and No. 15 hooks, while Al's are tied on No. 18 or No. 20 hooks. Charlie has a very sound theory about this. Sow bugs and shrimp examined in the stomachs of Letort trout in winter months are invariably of the smallest size; one-sixteenth-inch naturals as opposed to one-half-inch naturals are equivalent to hooks No. 18 or No. 20. Charlie reasons that winter-slowed metabolism necessitates smaller, easier-to-digest morsels. This is a boon to anglers. The smaller the lure the harder it is for trout to see it as a counterfeit. But it must be remembered that in these streams trout get a very long look, especially so during the cold months. So the fly tyer has exacting work cut out for him.

When I first compared Al Troth's facsimiles to the naturals, in a dripping wet clump of grass pulled from the Letort, I was incredulous at the likeness. Al Troth, as a professional tyer, can't be blamed for keeping his weapons secret, because, as Charlie says, "these are the best imitations I've ever seen." His shrimp bodies, for example, have the quality of translucency common to the natural. But the ties that have evolved among Letort regulars have also been effective. For the shrimp Charlie Fox recommends this tie: Tail: light honey hackle fibers. Body: 5X monofilament. Hackle: honey nylon. Hook: No. 20. Tying silk: honey.

Freshwater shrimp sometimes attach themselves in pairs. This is not a mating phenomenon, but it is common. So some tyers tie shrimp imitations in Siamese-twin fashion.

Charlie credits Wayne Leonard with the first effective sow bug imitation. The recommended tie is: Tail: none. Body: mixed fibers of buff and yellow nylon fur. Prepare as a mat and tie with doubled tying silk so as to avoid a "bunched" or "football" shaped body. Double silk promotes a flat profile. Trim bottom and top to further achieve flat profile. Hackle: none. Hook: No. 18. Tying silk: black.

The third member of the crustacea family that is a favorite trout food in limestone waters is the crayfish. On the Letort after dark on summer evenings large numbers of crayfish feed around and over elodea beds. For years Bill Blade's crayfish imitations—described in his book *Fishing Flies and Fly Tying*—has been considered by many to be the best. But when you are fishing for big, shy, nocturnal trout, it's important that the fly be delivered as noiselessly as possible. And heavy imitations like Blade's are prone to land with a "splat." Charlie Fox has found an effective answer in the old Neversink Skater. The long hackles render it large in appearance, but even when they are wet the fly lands lightly. With rod tip manipulation the hackle "breathes" (pulsates), giving the appearance of the swimming motion of the crayfish. A Neversink Skater looks nothing like a crayfish. But at nighttime true configuration is not nearly so important as size and action.

The size of any crayfish imitation, Charlie Fox believes, is an important and often overlooked factor. Like sow bugs, most crayfish found in Letort trout are small. Charlie reasons that trout find larger ones, with their tougher bodies and tentacles, less easy to masticate and digest than the smaller. So he uses Skaters rather than the more common, larger crayfish imitations.

Perhaps one of the most deadly flies in limestone waters is George Harvey's Horse Collar nymph, No. 20 and No. 22. When it is impossible to fish upstream with a dead-drift because of obstacles, this Harvey nymph, drifted downstream and retrieved in slow jerks, works wonders. It is commonly believed that trout take these flies for shrimp, because shrimp swim by jerking body movements. However, the Horse Collar nymph is good at any time, even when trout have varied food to choose from.

Charlie likes to tell of an experience involving his wife, Glad, which occurred in Big Spring when they were newlyweds. Glad, a complete neophyte, accompanied Charlie to assist in the removal of native brook trout for restocking in the Letort. He showed her how to retrieve a Horse Collar nymph and then began to prepare water containers. Immediately Glad caught a brookie and refused to take it off the hook. Charlie did so. Before he could return to his containers, Glad had another. Again Charlie came back to release it. A Keystone

Cops routine followed. Charlie was a long time in getting the containers filled with water but not with trout! Charlie's tie for George's nymph is: Tail: light ginger hackle fibers. Body: olive-green silk with olive-green color (chenille). Hackle: none. Hook: No. 20 or No. 22. Tying silk: olive green.

Probably the "hottest" midsummer terrestrial imitation for the limestone streams of south-central Pennsylvania is the cinnamon winged ant, developed on the Letort by Vince Marinaro. In working up the pattern, Vince had difficulty getting the right shade of cinnamon tying silk. But when he spotted the Fox's pony in the pasture one day, Vince found the perfect material for his cinnamon ant in the hair of the pony's tail. The tie simply involves the wrapping of a No. 22 hook with reddish-brown tying silk (since the pony's tail is no longer around) into a bulge fore and aft. In the wasp-waist center, a very narrow hackle spear of any color is tied.

One of the most fascinating tales of limestone innovating concerns Ernest Schwiebert, who is unquestionably one of the most experienced practitioners of grasshopper fishing in the fraternity of anglerwriters. During one of his early outings on the Letort almost 20 years ago, in the grasshopper season, Ernie became more displeased than the trout with the patterns he had used successfully in the West. He felt that the supremely selective trout of the Letort required a hopper imitation with better floatability and a more realistic profile. Ernie told Charlie Fox that he would return to his motel and try to concoct something better. He did just that. On the morrow, Ernie's new offering proved an immediate success. Ross Trimmer dubbed it the "Letort Hopper" and as such it has made history.

Ernie used yellow nylon rather than wool yarn to achieve maximum floatability in the body. Two upright turkey feathers represented legs, and the long wing was of natural bucktail. This, rather than the hackle, served to float the fly, either No. 8 or No. 10. For anyone interested in grasshopper fishing,

Ernie's article "Grasshopper Wind" in his *Rememberances of Rivers Past* is prerequisite reading.

That venerable, professional limestone fly tyer, Ed Shenk, developed an all-black version of the Letort grasshopper. A smaller edition is known as the Letort Cricket.

The magnitude of the contributions of south-central Pennsylvania's limestone school to the lore of trout angling can be grasped when they are compared to those made in the field of locomotion. Suppose that Isaac Watts were to discuss advances in propulsion over 200 years with Werner von Braun. I believe that Watts would be no more shocked than would Izaac Walton after comparing notes with Vince Marinaro and Charlie Fox. More's the pity that so few fly-tying anglers are involved in limestone practice—and innovating—for much remains to be done in the area of researching trout's feeding habits and their food forms, particularly terrestrials. Charlie Fox, for example, has discovered that lightning bugs and June bugs are fit fare for Letort trout. He's working now on representations.

But, some might say, compared to freestone streams, the limestone variety simply isn't available to the vast majority of fly fishermen. And if they were, the average fly angler would not be skillful enough to fish them successfully, let alone to tie those difficult imitations.

Those who find it impossible to fish over limestone trout will unnecessarily forgo a very large measure of enjoyment if they don't occasionally (when the season is right) fish the limestoners' best stand-bys—terrestrials on freestone water. For while it is a fact that alkaline water is required for aquatic crustacea, the more acid waters of freestone streams—particularly in summer months—entrap various terrestrial insects, the imitations of which were so assiduously developed by the dedicated limestoners of south-central Pennsylvania.

It's true that in relation to freestone streams, limestone waters are few and far between. But good limestone fisheries do exist in the far western and south-central states. So a large proportion of the nation's fly anglers are within convenient vacationing distances of limestone trout streams. And someone new to limestone trouting should definitely plan several days vacationing in the vicinity of the water to be fished. I've seen a lot of good freestone anglers drop into Carlisle to "wet a line" on the Yellow Breeches, Letort, or Big Springs over weekends and go away disillusioned.

On a classic limestone stream time should not be rushed. Whenever possible, newcomers should fish with experts, talk to them in depth. If this dictum is adhered to, the average freestone angler can expect some action, and in all likelihood he will have an enjoyable and memorable outing.

It is true that the smallest terrestrial and aquatic imitations can be tough to tie, particularly those requiring varied materials. A sensible and rewarding approach is to start with ones requiring few differing materials (the sow bug is a good example) and begin with a larger than intended size. After a few No. 14s, a No. 16 won't be too difficult. When you are satisfied with some No. 16s, step down to No. 18s. A No. 20 will not seem nearly so formidable a task as it would have had you tackled it from scratch.

TERRESTRIALS AND HAIR BUGS

Antelope, bighorn sheep, caribou, deer, elk, moose, and reindeer all have hollow hair and can be used for spun hair bugs. Hair from the neck and back of deer does not spin on as easily as the coarser hair in the sides. It is always wise for the beginner to select the coarsest hair. The size thread one must use is determined by the size of bunches of hair to be spun on the hook. On small trout-size terrestrials (No. 16 to No. 18), one may use 4–0; on larger bass bugs where large bunches of hair is used one may use thread as large as A.

We will only illustrate how to spin on the hair and use diagrams showing the shape to clip the hair for trout-size terrestrials. Where tails are required, they of course would be tied on first. I believe that even the neophyte tyer will have no trouble duplicating any hair bug once he has acquired the knack of spinning on the hair.

Diagram #1 shows how to hold the hair. Start with a larger size hook (4–6) and practice spinning on a bare shank. Follow this procedure:

First secure the thread at the bend of the hook. Now cut small section, about half the diameter of a lead pencil, and hold as diagrammed between thumb and finger. Bring thread loosely up between thumb and hair over the top and down the other side between hair and index finger. Next start to repeat the first step, and as thread is brought over top, start to tighten up as you release pressure on hair. As you tighten up on the thread you spread the hair out fan shape by shifting thumb and finger. Hair should spin completely around hook shank. Make several more tight turns through hair and bring thread up in front of hair. Now hold thumb and finger of left hand at rear of spun hair and with thumb and finger of right hand push hair back so it is compact. Next wind several turns of tying thread around front of hair to hold in place. Repeat this process until hook is covered. Secure by half hitches or whip finish. Now you can practice clipping the bug to desired shape.

You should practice spinning enough hair on the shank of the hook until you are satisfied you have mastered the technique. If you tie a bug by using the above practice method, the hair after it is clipped will tend

108

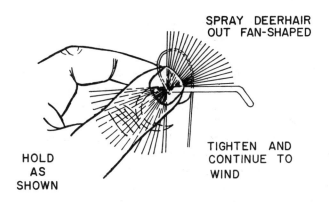

SPRAY DEERHAIR
OUT FAN-SHAPED

HOLD
AS
SHOWN

TIGHTEN AND
CONTINUE TO
WIND

DIAGRAM 1

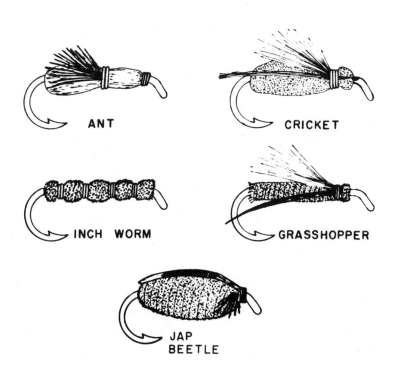

ANT

CRICKET

INCH WORM

GRASSHOPPER

JAP
BEETLE

DIAGRAM 2

to twist on the hook. The next step is to take some quick-drying cement, cover shank of hook with it, and start tying thread back of eye and wind smoothly back to bend of hook. Learn to spin over the thread base. This will probably take a little more practice but should not take very long if one has practiced enough spinning on a bare shank. When you spin the hair on the thread base it should not twist on the hook. If you want to add wings or legs on the terrestrials they may be tied on after the hair is clipped to desired shape. I suggest you purchase copies of the more important patterns. You should be able to duplicate them all and perhaps add a little something new! Diagram #2 illustrates the shape of the more common terrestrials.

Don't be afraid to innovate. Who knows, you may come up with a bug that will be an all-time great!

TERRESTRIALS

Name	Hook	Body	Hackle	Wing	Legs
Jassid (Marinaro)	#18 or #20	orange silk	ginger	jungle cock (tied as a roof)	
Jap Beetle (Harvey)	#12 or #14	black deer hair (clipped)		jungle cock (cemented as roof)	black duck or goose quill fibers
Cinnamon Ant	#20 or #22	amber or cinnamon horsehair	any color wound in "wasp waist"	thorax tie	
Green Oak Worm	#12 or #14	green deer hair (clipped)			
Grass-hopper	#8 2X long or #10 2X long	yellow deer hair (clipped)		deer hair tuft on top	dyed red duck or goose quill fibers

110

George Harvey, the professional's expert,
at his tying bench.

A view of George Harvey and his tremendous
inventory of tying materials in his specially-
built hideaway tying room.

(right) A Pocono trout falls for one of George's little Sulphurs.
(Trout Fisherman's Digest, DBI Books, Inc.)

The late John Stauffer, the author's mentor, with his guide and a freshly caught grisle on New Brunswick's Mirimichi River. *(The Flyfisher)*

Samuel C. Slaymaker III hooks a trout on one of his first streamers on the Poconos' Brodheads.

The author with a 20-inch, three-pound native brown trout taken on Spruce Creek with one of George Harvey's Yellow Maribu streamers. (*Trout Fisherman's Digest,* DBI Books, Inc.)

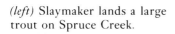

(left) Slaymaker lands a large trout on Spruce Creek.

The Dean of the Letort River, Charles K. Fox, near the bronze plaque that the Cumberland County chapter of Trout, Unlimited placed on the bank of the Letort in his honor. (*Trout Fisherman's Digest*, **DBI Books, Inc.**)

Charlie Fox examines water weeds for natural sow bugs and freshwater shrimp.

The Dean of the Letort landing a Letort brown. (*Trout Fisherman's Digest*, **DBI Books, Inc.**)

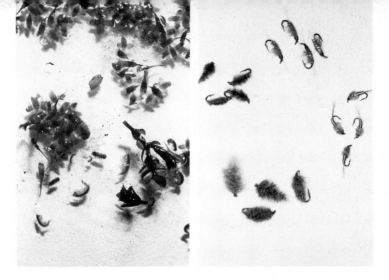

A comparison of real and artificial freshwater shrimp and
sow bugs: *(left)* photographed alive among water weeds;
(right, clockwise from top) smaller shrimp, tied by Al Troth;
horse-collar nymph imitations tied by George Harvey;
large sow bug imitations tied by Wayne Leonard;
and Al Troth's smaller sow bug imitations.

On the Letort in January, Slaymaker drifts a freshwater shrimp.

On the west branch of Pennsylvania's Brandywine, angler-author Jim Bashline examines May fly life to determine which nymph imitation to dig from his fly box.

Angler-author Don DuBois, about to beach a stream-bred trout on the Poconos' Brodheads. *(Fishing World)*

Sam Black teases a weighted nymph in Pocono fast waters.

One of Ken Depoe's fly-tying students about to net a chunky rainbow on the reclaimed Donegal stream. *(Fishing World)*

5. *"Over Many Years I Do Believe That I've Had as Much Fun with Flies as with Trout"*

—THE LATE JOHN STAUFFER

ABOVE THE DESK on which I write these lines hangs a framed black-and-white photograph of a fly rod, flanked by four glistening brown trout, on a rhododendron-draped boulder. The fish fell to the first Royal Coachman dry fly I tied, almost 30 years ago. This particular fly became instrumental in my discovery of a whimsical sort of avocation that is conducive to enhancing the contemplative powers of fly-tying anglers. The picture on the study wall and the fly itself constantly jog memories of its almost magical powers and the bizarre train of events to which they gave rise.

My Quill Gordon dries were not matching an afternoon hatch on the Brodheads in April 1953. I didn't feel too badly, though, since trout were not taking on top and hard-fished nymphs and streamers failed to evoke much action below. There seemed nothing better to do during my remaining hour than to see how well my first Royal Coachman would float. Lovingly, I removed it from the box and remembered with a grin the unmerciful ribbing I'd taken from my father while it was still in the vise.

The parents had come for a Sunday dinner during the preceding winter. I was applying the whip finish as "S.C." (my father) entered the room, delivering himself of remarks deprecatory of fly fishermen. A true believer in worms (he hadn't fished in over 50 years), S.C. could not bring himself to believe that artificial flies actually catch fish. Nor could he be convinced that many fly anglers release most of their catches. In short, he believed all fly anglers to be poseurs and many of them liars.

Throughout dinner I regaled S.C. with this fly's history—how it evolved from the vise of one of Queen Victoria's coachmen. The tale was calculated to intrigue him, and it did—well enough to bring on a truce he guaranteed would be lasting so long as I brought him trout (he loved trout baked in wine) taken on this fly and so attested to by me on a Bible.

I was not at all sanguine about delivering on the promise while preparing to tempt those listless Brodhead trout with my beautiful Royal Coachman. But in short order it was taken by a small brookie. A few minutes later a chunky brown tore into the fly—literally, as I discovered when I extricated it from the toothy jaws of this 14-inch fish.

So the rear peacock herl was trailing, but it didn't look too bad: I kept on casting. I soon caught and released a small brookie. Now the fly was beginning to look ratty. Fearing that a replacement might break my lucky streak, I continued casting. As the fly became more disheveled it took more fish. They struck on very nearly every cast. I don't know how many were landed in an hour, but when I stopped fishing the now hopelessly mauled Royal Coachman my creel held four exquisite browns, all over a foot long.

I arranged the still-life tableau on a boulder as artistically as I knew how. The battered fly was placed on a trout's head. But I was too excited. The shadow of a rhododendron leaf, the print revealed, had blotted it out.

The fish were delivered to S.C. His Bible was not handy, so I took my oath on a Presbyterian prayerbook. His expression was one of belief, or at least near belief. He never again denigrated fly fishermen with the old vehemence.

Somehow I could not make myself dispose of the ruined fly. Lord knew I could never use it again. Still, it was my first tie of this very famous pattern. And its effectiveness was so phenomenal as to defy repetition. It had to be saved, I thought, as was my first ever fly, the Squirrel Tail Streamer that caught the big native. The two flies were placed in an acetate fly box, deep in a wall closet.

During succeeding years when one of my flies distinguished itself by catching an especially nice fish (or a lot of them) I found myself "retiring" the fly to the acetate box. After a decade of fishing my own flies almost exclusively, there were three acetate boxes full of badly chewed flies of all sorts and conditions. For reasons that escape me now—or maybe there was no reason besides too many retired flies—I decided to apply more stringent qualifications for retirement. At first, each fly that had taken a decent fish was retired. Then I upped the requirement to several fish per fly. Soon a more systematic method was arrived at: A fly could be retired only after a minimum of 12 legal trout and a maximum of 20.

Now this might seem unduly arbitrary and utterly nonsensical, but I had reasons. Were I to retire each fly when it took a trout, my "used" collection would have become unwieldy. When trout are taking a given fly well, it's senseless to take time to change to another of the same pattern after only a dozen fish are landed. But the chances of losing a fly increase in direct proportion to the number of fish it takes; so 20 to a fly seemed a safe maximum, while the minimum of 12 seemed enough to insure indelible memories that a glance at said fly could rekindle. And this minimum assured at least a moderate number of retirees at the end of each season.

Over the years these limits proved convenient. What with giveaways, losses, and those occasional ties that came apart, I rarely had more than 25 retirements per year.

But how to relive those on-stream memories when my retirees were snuggled in an acetate box, stored in a wall closet? Seventeen years and 531 retirements later, thanks to my wife, Sally, the question stopped dogging me.

We needed a low, sofa-bordering coffee table for our living room. Our other furniture is Early American, but this table had to be contemporary, since a convertible antique seemed too hard to find. So it was bound to clash.

On Labor Day, 1965, I was accosted in the act of storing the past season's retirees. "Whatever are you going to do with those things?" sniffed Sal. "They'll just draw moths."

I insisted that moth flakes were put in the box each year.

"Well, they're useless and should be pitched," she went on.

Deeply hurt, I heatedly reminded her that her aunt was about to pitch some of Theodore Gordon's original streamer patterns when Dr. Jimmy Trotter died; that, thank heavens, I had stopped her, and that it was a darn good thing I had, being as how they resulted in my history of streamer angling in America for the late Arnold Gingrich (in *Esquire*, May 1962, and *Esquire's Book of Fishing*, Harper & Row).

I was reminded that I was no Theodore Gordon. True enough, but the remark stung. A tense silence ensued as Sal's impatient glance fastened on the wall closet. Then she turned and murmured, "The Gordon flies are proper American antiques. Mount them in a coffee table and you'll get a kind of historic flavor in a contemporary piece—different, anyway."

An excited rejoinder to the effect that this was the answer for my flies, too, did not exactly send Sal. But she went along. Milt Eby, whose shop in nearby Paradise, Pennsylvania, reproduces Early American furniture, was commissioned. We wanted nothing of a phony, rustic nature. It was to be plain.

The result is as pleasing as it is practical. The wood is Pennsylvania wild cherry, and the lines are clean and of a colonial flavor. The table measures 22 inches wide by 48 inches long and 18 inches high. The frame around the recessed area is 3 1/2 inches wide, and the blue velveteen liner is set in the

114

recess, 7/8 inches deep. To facilitate rearrangement the flush and snug-fitting glass top can easily be removed.

After-dinner coffee has ceased to be a hurried pick-me-up, gulped prior to a few hours of writing in the study. I now linger over it, dreamily conjuring long-gone memories of bright water and rising trout. Each fly suggests different ones, many hazily at first. But familiarity has bred a tableau, in some instances a series of them, which time can now no longer pale.

Our coffee table has afforded another matchless blessing.

The only thing I used to loath more than going to a cocktail party was giving one. But now I can't contain myself until sufficient obligations dictate our next pay-off, the pattern of which has become easily predictable: Early birds drift to an end-of-the-hall buffet. A pile-up soon spills over to the living room. Sibilant silks and sloshing ice cubes meld with a swelling henhouselike din, soon to be pierced by an ejaculatory "very creative" or a breathless "most unusual" and inevitably at least one giggling "how quaint."

Then I back modestly into the limelight and point out the table's central display, the ancient Gordon streamers—genuine American antiques, indigenous contributions to an art form otherwise lifted in toto from England. The more observant note that my dressings appear worn. I comment that this feature distinguishes them from a mass purchase of superior Abercrombie & Fitch ties, so proper for framings and paperweights—and coffee tables—for mine have actually taken trout!

I single out the Squirrel Tail. Its birth and baptism are recounted. Then comes my original Little Brown Trout Bucktail, Streamerette ties (after John S. Wise Jr.'s original patterns) and the first variant "seasonal" dry flies. Sounds of silk and ice recede with thinning smoke. Only three or four are left from the original 10 or a dozen listeners—mostly anglers or potential converts to the fly. (The table has made four in the past year.)

We sprawl around the table with refilled glasses and talk fishing. I don't have to dominate the scene anymore. Invariably, someone in the group has had great days with me and one or more of the patterns. Believe me, it's all too soon when bedeviling wives drag the participants homeward and racket subsides, blending on night air with crunching gravel and humming engines.

Since there are over a hundred flies in the table, the risk of rehashing the same experiences twice with a given guest is not great. Before the next round of parties, though, I take the precautionary measure of giving the present arrangement a rest. After all, there are four hundred more trout flies in the wall closet hurting to be heard from!

My inherited bent toward frugality is probably responsible for a use I've found for the beat-up flies which aren't qualified for retirement. They are fished again—but never over sophisticated trout in civilized waters.

It's a well-known axiom that naïve wilderness trout fall easier prey to attractor flies than to deceivers and that the reverse is true with the wary trout of hard-fished waters. In the upper reaches of Quebec and Newfoundland I've also discovered that mangy flies of all kinds catch as many or more fish than those in mint condition. Obviously, their rugged appearance enhances their attracting powers.

Years ago, when I was fishing a wilderness lake in Newfoundland for native brook trout, my guide and I were trolling Gray Ghost streamers from a canoe with good results. My early home tie, which was not well put together, began to unravel. Trout went mad for my streamer, while the intact store-bought Gray Ghost of my guide performed with the same regularity that it had earlier.

The Gray Ghost is a good streamer to troll in lakes because a little rod-tip action activates well its large, supple flank feathers, resulting in an attracting action superior to that of bucktail streamers. In lakes, of course, the angler has to supply the action, since current is lacking. In good condition our Ghosts served us better than the Mickey Finns trolled earlier. But when my Gray Ghost trailed a flank feather and body ribbing, it became as killing a lure as I've ever fished.

In wild waters I've also found this to be true with nymphs, wets, and dries. So, when I journey to wilderness areas a collection of beat-up flies always goes along.

Perhaps my most exciting experience involving the use of derelict dry flies occurred in the wilds of Alaska. Since the exotic and rare arctic grayling was involved, this yarn bears telling in its entirety.

Those who never have fished in Alaska are prone to dream about its king-size rainbow trout: huge, torpedolike Chinook salmon—and their millions of silver and crimson cousins clogging the cold, cascading rivers of this pristine, snow-capped never-never land. Alaska, we tell ourselves, is the El Dorado of trophy fish. We vow to take ours there some day.

After long years of waiting, my opportunity came in July 1973. While on a business trip to Seattle, I contacted Mike Hershberger, one of Alaska's best-known guides. I had read Mike's articles and was anxious to meet him. He had scheduled a float trip with a Chicago lawyer and fly fisherman, Zeamore Ader, and he suggested that I join them.

When I got to Anchorage I was happy to learn that my firm's Alaska agents had arranged to have one of their representatives—Gary Schmitt, a onetime Oregon guide—come along. Mike hired pilot Dave Klosterman, "Alaskan Bush Carrier" of Anchorage, to fly us 70 miles northwest of Anchorage to the Talachulitna River.

We loaded Dave's Cessna 206 and took off from the Anchorage float plane port in midafternoon. In minutes we were winging over trackless Alaskan hinterlands—a seemingly endless blue-green carpet of spruce, birch, and tamarack, splotched here and there with emerald patches of swampland.

117

While skirting the snow-capped peaks of the Chigmit range we sighted a gauzelike haze on the northwestern horizon. Mike said that extensive Siberian forest fires were responsible. I felt an instantaneous thrill as I realized that we were certain of wilderness fishing of the first order.

After an hour we landed on a smooth stretch of the Talachulitna River, unloaded our gear, inflated the rubber raft—dubbed by Mike "Catadromous" (going to sea)—and made ready for our float.

The Talachulitna is roughly 50 miles long. It rises in the foothills of the Chigmit Mountains and flows into the Squentna River, which enters the sea near Anchorage. Our starting point was 2,100 feet above sea level. We planned to float approximately 20 miles to the pick-up point, about 60 feet above sea level. This steep decline would occasion "some fairly swift water," Mike said, but he noted that it was broken by long, smooth stretches so that our descent "wouldn't be too rough." The river is shallow, so there would be little danger from upsets. Mike was equipped to repair minor tears in the raft, but we could have problems with large gashes, not easy to avoid in the rock-ridden, swift-flowing Talachulitna, then at its midsummer low. Were we to be "shipwrecked," we could camp on an easily seen spit of land until the rescue fly boys from Elmendortf Air Force Base in Anchorage could rescue us.

A bright sun was still high in the sky when we pushed off around 6:00 P.M. The raft soon drifted into a majestic, curving stretch of river, briskly riffled and broken by long, crystal-clear glides. Fish were beginning to dimple. Mike said they were feeding on mosquitoes—their main insect fare, since Alaskan waters do not rear much aquatic fly life—and suggested that we try a few casts.

Save the odd deep pool, this river is almost entirely wadable. So Zeamore Ader (whom we called "Z"), Gary Schmitt, and I slid into the water while Mike beached the raft. I dropped a Queen of the Waters dry fly into a swirling midstream pocket. A foot-long streak of silver-tinged lavender arched gracefully over the bounding fly.

"Grayling!" I shouted happily as the plunging fish vanished in a splash of white water. He jumped again. Then came a dash followed by a surface display. Bringing the fish to my boots, I experienced one of the keenest thrills in all my years of fly fishing: my first arctic grayling, a fish renowned in literature and favored by poets and anglers. I first savored the sight of his subdued, yet beautifully colored flanks and the large, speckled, saillike dorsal fin, then gently removed the fly, and the fish was quickly lost in crystal-clear currents.

I loved this dainty fish all the more for its total lack of sophistication. A beat-up old dry fly worked as well as the Queen of Waters. An even more mangled no-name, long-hackled skater produced well too. So I vowed that I would continue to use my supply of worn-out dry flies. For a half hour the group tangled with grayling. Mike caught the largest, a two-pounder. As we started back to the raft "Z" shouted that he was into "something big," a sky-writing rainbow of 18 inches. "Z" fought it for a good 10 minutes before beaching it.

A float of a couple of miles brought us to the one and only portage. After an hour of tugging, hauling, and crawling over precipitous rocks, we entered a gorge of immense proportions through which the river coursed in a series of deep pools.

"Here's where we'll find the biggest rainbows," Mike promised. He knew what he was talking about. Gary hooked one of more than 20 inches; Mike soon had one of almost 30 inches, and vicious fighters they were. All struck deep down. With the dearth of fly life, these large trout feed on small fish, and that's what they must have taken our most effective streamer—the Skykomish Sunrise, weighted—to be.

Not liking weight, I eschewed it and paid the penalty of catching only a "small" rainbow of 16 inches. But Mike was insistent. "You've got to get down in this fast water for the big ones. Without some weight, you're lost!"

Reluctantly fumbling for a split shot, I glanced downriver. Under a cherry-red sunset I spotted rise forms. More grayling! The temptation to throw my old dry flies at them was irresistible. I hiked a quarter of a mile down to the shallow stretches where grayling were playing. While the others continued to catch large rainbows until they became arm-weary, I caught grayling beyond count. Always there was that arching, out-of-water take—a jump or two, runs and surface wallops. But repetitious action brought no surfeit of pleasure.

That night we camped on a wide expanse of graveled shoreline, devoid of trees, thanks to the past winter's gigantic ice floes, which had gouged the riverbanks, uprooting trees and vegetation. The now bone-dry tree limbs made ideal firewood.

We retired after 11:00 P.M. It was dark now, but not deeply so because of the ever-lingering afterglow. Periodically there came from the river the sound of erupting water. Large Chinook salmon were moving through on their upriver spawning run.

The next morning dawned overcast and raw with the threat of rain, but the day grew warmer under bursts of intermittent sunshine. Shortly after resuming our drift, we entered a series of rapids. Mike assured us that they were tame compared to those of some other Alaskan rivers, but for neophyte river runners like "Z" Ader and myself, these rough stretches still produced some palpitations of the heart. Mike perched on the bow, feet outstretched, paddle at the ready—the better to slip the raft around the myriad protruding rocks. Gary steered from the stern. Our speed was often brisk, so they had to be uncommonly dexterous, and they were. We had no upsets as we raced down those roaring cascades, and we emerged from the boiling rapids into placid water with not a single tear in the raft.

After lunching on smoked salmon, we fished for a couple of hours. Again my colleagues were mesmerized by deep water and lunker rainbows, while I fished for the delicate grayling in the riffles. I still can't account for the spell this fish cast on me, because the grayling were not at all selective. My ratty dry flies continued to work wonders. Even rainbows—the smaller ones in shallow water—rose with total abandon to my worst offerings, some of which were lost to fairly heavy fish. Had the trip lasted a day or two longer, I could easily have used up my supply.

Late in the afternoon we drifted through long runs of varied species of migrating Pacific salmon. We caught some jack salmon, young Chinooks, on streamers. Mike told us that Chinooks are not readily caught here on flies, and we found this to be true. Our catches consisted mainly of grayling and rainbows.

With the approach of dusk we beached the raft on a graveled promontory and made camp. An hour of fabulous fishing followed. We killed a couple of rainbows and a grayling for Mike to filet and cook for the evening repast.

Because of the day's frequent and rugged bouts of wading and boat dragging through the shallow water, we bedded down and were soon asleep.

The last day dawned cold and cloudy. After breakfast and some fishing, we pushed off. The water was extremely low, and we had as much trouble going downstream as the salmon, flailing and foundering all about us, were having in their ascent. A lot of wading on slippery boulders ensued. A welcome noon-hour rest came on a long gravel bar, where we lunched on ham and smoked salmon. Later, in a long, deep pool, we battled heroic-sized rainbows for a couple of hours. Then came the last leg of the float.

Late on the third day we spotted the first sign of civilization (also our pick-up point), an observation tower in mid-river from which Fish and Game Department relay teams count migrating salmon. Aching and dog-tired, we unloaded the raft, deflated it, and waited for Dave Klosterman's plane, scheduled for 4:30 P.M. He was there on the dot. It was the end of a lifelong dream that had come true at last; and I'd discovered an exciting but rather expensive way to use up old trout flies!

The coffee-table exhibit is probably responsible for my lack of enthusiasm for flies mounted in jewelry, paperweights, cocktail glasses, shadow boxes, and the like. The more striking the ties, the more annoyed I become. They represent a waste of materials and energy. A fly, I'm convinced, should be fished and *then* displayed. I'm prepared to bet that used trout flies mounted, say, in tie clips would be fabulous sellers to the outdoorsy trade—if they were packaged with chits attesting to their prowess! "This well-chewed Quill Gordon," one might read, "was used by Joe Doaks to deck a 23-inch brown trout on the Neversink on June 18, 1975." I've often mulled over the idea of using my old flies in this way. The supply could easily be augmented by swapping new ties with other anglers for old ones having stories to tell.

Years ago, when I received the bill for my first tying kit, ordered by John Stauffer, I figured that I was into an expensive pastime. Even in those days good, stiff, dry-fly necks came at a high price. I was happy to discover eventually that average fly tyers can use one for a very long time and that they are the only big ticket items required. I soon learned, too, that satisfactory materials are free and easy to come by in many unlikely places.

There are, of course, the obvious sources of supply such as my game bag. Pheasant feathers are always in abundance; occasionally there is quail, grouse, and woodcock. On goose and duck hunts on Maryland's eastern shore I always lay in goodly supplies of feathers for my wing cutters. Our Amish farmer's boys trap muskrat and shoot rabbits, squirrels and groundhogs, so plenty of fur for bodies comes off our farm. Deer-hunting friends keep me in bucktail.

Then there's Sal's knitting bag—an always ready source of

122

varicolored yarns. My almost compulsive collecting of bits and pieces of woolen stemmed from a bizarre tying incident involving John Stauffer and a killing salmon fly, "Herman's Sweater."

For many years John fished a stretch of the Mirimichi River leased by a tough, World War I Canadian Guardsman, Herman Campbell. During one evening of wassailing, John and Herman's other guests hit on the idea of tying a wet fly from his aged and weatherbeaten woolen sweater. The following tie resulted: No. 6 or No. 8 hook; reddish-brown wool body; ribbed gold tinsel (or wire); orange tail (feather); throat, red hackle barbs; wings, black hair. On the morrow the fly took salmon well. Over succeeding years "Herman's Sweater" became a successful and well-known pattern in the Maritimes. Whether or not the sweater was totally cannibalized, genuine "Herman's Sweaters" eventually became as scarce as hen's teeth. When I was Herman's guest years later, he gave me an original. It produced a grisle before I lost it in a tail-walking salmon.

Friends in all walks have put me down as some kind of a nut because of my insatiable desire to latch onto oddball materials, sometimes in situations that my loved ones find embarrassing. Once, at a very plush dinner party a bejeweled dowager spoke at length about alterations she planned for her wardrobe of furs. I asked for the trimmings, explained my needs (which led to a dissertation on fly tying which fascinated the lady but bored the others), and secured permission to panhandle from her tailor—all of which greatly upset Sal and my mother. But I got more than a lifetime supply of mink and raccoon, perfect for a wide range of nymph and wet fly bodies. Later, when a friend inherited a chinchilla ranch, I became the recipient of chinchilla hair, useful for mixing with bucktail hair for streamers and streamerettes.

Naturally, my hoard of fly-tying materials became gargantuan. There was far and away too much for one sometime tyer

123

to consume. So I began to thin the supply periodically by making donations to our Trout, Unlimited chapter's fly-tying classes and raffles.

Giving one's flies to other anglers is nowhere near as satisfying as helping others to tie their own. The tyer who gives his time to do so contributes greatly to the cause of trout conservation, a dramatic case in point being the accomplishments of Ken Depoe, a high-school teacher from Mt. Joy, Pennsylvania.

Singing riffles, diamond-clear water and tail-walking trout are the attributes of untracked wilderness streams. Yet Donegal Creek, traversing the tourist-clogged Pennsylvania Dutch country, a scant mile from where the main route between Lancaster and Harrisburg bisects the borough of Mt. Joy, has these hallmarks in sufficient quantities to make it very much like the real thing.

As incongruous as the locale is its topography. The Donegal meanders through luxuriant farmland that is markedly deficient in tree cover, a prerequisite of most trout streams as a check to eroding topsoil.

Time was when the stream's surroundings presented a tableau more akin to trout-water norms. In pre-Revolutionary days timber predominated over sparse clearings. The then tumbling, white-water stream rose three and a half miles west of present-day Mt. Joy from a series of crystalline springs. Here in 1740 the Scots-Irish settlers built Donegal Presbyterian Church. As they moved west, the region was taken over by German farmers, who deforested and cultivated the rich soil.

The church still stands. Fluttering flags by weathered tombstones set in neatly manicured oak groves attest to its status as a Revolutionary War shrine. Until three years ago, however, the Donegal was anything but a proper trout stream—not that it was polluted, nor, thanks to the springs, had the water temperature become too high. But it was badly silted. Current-deflecting boulders, rocks, and gravel beds were long since covered by eroded soil. The flow lacked sufficient aeration to furnish trout necessary oxygen. And the dearth of gravel rendered aquatic fly life virtually nonexistent. Spawning beds were nil.

Restoration of much of the Donegal to its pristine state resulted from the vision, dedication, and labor of Ken Depoe. A dedicated angler and fly tyer, Ken, like most of his fraternity, felt constrained to win converts to it. His vocation presented a built-in opportunity. As an extracurricular course—with no remuneration to himself—he started a fly-tying class at his high school. It was an immediate success.

The logical next step was to develop budding fly anglers. But where to use the flies? Trout water was too distant for class members under driving age—the vast majority. Ken knew enough about stream improvement to think the Donegal might be his answer, but an improvement project would take a lot of time. His duties teaching and as wrestling coach left him precious little. So he huddled with the fly-tying class, and as a result each boy enthusiastically volunteered for year-round stream work.

Ken delved deeply into writings on stream improvement and sought out the waterway patrolman, Sam Hall, who offered valuable advice during the planning stages and later became excited enough to work with the group on his own time. He also served as an excellent source for the technical information made available by the Pennsylvania Fish Commission.

Sam Hall first recommended that permission for the project be secured from landowners who would be involved. The group stressed that stream improvement would enhance the aesthetic value, hence the worth of their lands, and that flooding and the consequent loss to topsoil could be minimized. They offered fence repair and maintenance, thus promising to reduce the farmers' work load. They pledged to respect property. The clincher was a reminder that property owners would be contributing to the betterment of youth and the conservation of a valuable natural resource in a historical setting.

Owners of land bordering two contiguous miles of stream consented. The primary objective was the creation of a channel with sufficient current to promote flushing action. Silt could then be washed from the stream bed. A series of gabions (wire-encased and anchored rock piles that jut at angles from bankside), dams, and stone deflectors were planned to accomplish the flushing action.

Within two weeks came the first in a series of gratifying phenomena. Along the mud-clogged bottom of the developing channel a streak of yellow-ocher appeared and widened by the day. Here was gravel—the key to the stream's rejuvenation. There was hope now for increased aquatic fly life and, as the clearing action reached bankside shallows, for potential spawning beds for the trout.

During the initial stage an adequate supply of rocks was found along the stream, while logs for dams were scrounged from neighbors and friends. But as the job recommenced the following year, it became obvious that the need for materials dictated a major panhandling effort. Ken Depoe, Sam Hall, and interested friends sought contributions from area businessmen whose trade answered a specific need. Of crucial help, for example, was a local quarry. Not only was much needed rock supplied; it was transported to streamside in company trucks.

Throughout another summer Ken and his faithful crew sweated at their back-wrenching, knuckle-scraping job. More silt was rinsing away, and the current deflectors were aerating water. Glides whispered over shallow log dams and broke on gravel beds into singing riffles that gurgled into eddying pools against the jutting gabions and deflectors. The Donegal was beginning to look and sound like a trout stream again.

Still, the patience of teenagers can be short-lived. Ken's group had put in many consecutive months of drudgery. Ken thought that interest might flag should the wetting of their flies be too long delayed. His rumination bore an idea certain to give his boys their second wind, however: They would raise their own trout!

The class chipped in and bought 300 brown and rainbow trout fingerlings. A farmer friend of Ken's permitted his springhouse to be used for trout rearing. Cared for by the class, the fish averaged 9 to 11 inches in nine months' time, thanks to an amazingly rich natural food supply in the spring's raceway—shrimp, sow bugs, and aquatic insect life. The trout were distributed in the improved stretch, and new fingerlings were bought for the springhouse.

The possibility that those many months of drudgery might undermine enthusiasm was now nil. For Ken quickly imparted to the class casting skill sufficient to catch the scrappy trout. And he stressed the use of streamers, since they're the easiest flies for beginners to fish. Even jaded experts sometimes find it hard to stifle a gasp when, on teasing streamers down riffles and retrieving them through glides and glassy pockets, they glimpse the blood-red flash of striking rainbows and feel their thumping takes. The thrill was much greater for these raw novices.

But Ken's efforts had created more than 21 fly anglers; 21 conservationists were born. They were taught that flies—because they cause minimal injury to fish—made it possible for them to return most of their catches to the stream.

As the project was extended, more fish than the group could raise were required. So they asked if the Pennsylvania Fish Commission would include the completed portion of the Donegal in its Fly Fish Only program. But work had not progressed to the point where the stream could meet established qualifications.

Undeterred, Ken Depoe's force expanded the project to cover a full two miles. Anxious to stimulate growth of aquatic fly life, the group made frequent field trips in search of May fly nymphs. From the Yellow Breeches in nearby Cumberland County they brought nymphs to the Donegal in water-filled containers. As the stream continued to purge itself of silt, a notable increase in aquatic flies occurred. Since the Hendrickson, which is common to the Yellow Breeches, was among the varied species, Ken felt that the transplants were at least partially responsible for the gratifying results.

The need for construction materials and money for out-of-pocket expenditures grew as the stretch of completed stream lengthened. And as the community was benefiting and would continue to do so, it seemed to those involved in the effort that it should be formally organized. Thus was born the Donegal Fish and Conservation Association. Regular donations were solicited throughout Lancaster County. The response was highly successful. An area newspaper featured a pictorial spread. Ken was interviewed on my friend Harry Allaman's well-known regional TV show, "Call of the Outdoors." Anglers from as distant as the Baltimore area began to appear on the stream.

In mid-October 1966 I was in a business meeting. Word had been left that I would take no phone calls, but the office switchboard girl broke in: "Waterway Patrolman Sam Hall calling. He insists on getting you."

Sam was phoning from a booth in Mt. Joy, still in boots and wet through from a morning in the stream.

"I've shocked the Donegal," he said breathlessly. "The original planting has survived! Some are going just shy of 14 inches long." Eleven months later Sam got me out of another meeting with word that stream-bred fingerling rainbows were turned up by a shocking. The Donegal was now truly reborn.

During the summer of 1967 a group of area trout angler–conservationists formed a chapter of Trout, Unlimited and elected Ken Depoe president. Fittingly, it was named the Donegal Chapter of Trout, Unlimited. Using the Donegal project as a guide, the group has begun another stream reclamation project in southeastern Pennsylvania.

The Pennsylvania Fish Commission eventually named the two miles of reclaimed Donegal Creek a Fly Fish Only stretch and included it in the state stocking program. On Memorial Day, 1967, Governor Shafer visited the project, congratulated the Donegal Conservation Association and received an honorary life membership.

Those present at the ceremony might have pondered that this stream, like Scrooge's Christmas, had been possessed of three ghosts—in this instance one of a delightful past, another of uncertain present, and finally one of a promising future. Its first two ghosts represent, in microcosm, the lives of too many American trout streams. Like the Donegal, they once flowed clear, strong, and deep. Now, encroaching civilization renders them clouded, weak, and flat. But if they are not hopelessly polluted—many aren't as yet—and if they possess springs cool enough to maintain temperatures no higher than the low 70s, they do have the ghost of a bright future. All that's needed to conjure it up is more people like Ken Depoe.

Thankfully, his tribe has increased phenomenally in recent years. Virtually all of the burgeoning satellite organizations of Trout, Unlimited and the Fly Fishing Federation are now sponsoring fly-tying courses, which invariably result in more stream-improvement projects and increasing numbers of fly fishermen. So, of all the offshoot hobbies provided by fly tying, none is as pleasurable and rewarding as helping to create a fly-fishing lobby.

EPILOGUE—*The Odyssey of a Fly-Angling Johnny Appleseed*

H. L. MENCKEN'S DICTUM that "it is impossible to underestimate the intelligence of the American people" is becoming more and more obvious. A cult of careless self-indulgence has waxed stronger of late, and this is all too evident to nature lovers who find wood, field, and stream despoiled by litterers. Some industrial polluters are deservedly getting lumps for their longtime pollution of the environment. But precious little progress has been made with the littering populace at large, particularly with many so-called outdoorsmen and sportsmen. I am unalterably convinced that fly fishermen, by virtue of the enlightened aesthetic outlook that the imitation of nature gives rise to, are very rarely found among the ranks of the fish hogs and the litterbugs. Proof positive of this contention can be seen on the stretch of the Donegal that was set aside for fly fishing only some five or six years ago. The stream is litterfree—ironically so, since the fly area is much more heavily used than the unregulated water. The fly fishermen don't appear in numbers of any consequence until later in the season. Then they use the fly-fish-only water hard through the end of the season. The unregulated water, however, is frequented early in the season

130

by the put-and-take bait fishermen, and as one traverses the unregulated portion of the stream one finds beer and soft-drink cans, the inevitable forksticks to hold bait-casting or spinning rods, cigarette wrappers, and debris of all sorts.

Thanks to the growing numbers of fly fishermen, more water is becoming regulated. But, since state conservation agencies throughout the country are overseen by politicians, fishery men feel constrained to do the bidding of the well-organized "sportsmen's clubs," which have a lot of political muscle. As fly fishing grows in popularity, the power of the sportsmen's clubs tends to wane. Come the happy day when the fly-fishing lobby becomes dominant, the trend toward natural angling and the conservation of trout will become a fully established fact.

The growth of fly-tying classes is instrumental in bringing this millennium to fruition. Recently I came up with the idea of making a movie based on *Simplified Fly Fishing*, which we could show to our fly-tying classes during their last tying sessions. The idea was simply to show the new tyers that fishing their flies wasn't all that tough. As it turned out, the movie ended up being used for "sportsmen" groups as well, and, if I may say so, quite effectively.

Lights dim, a hush settles over the smoke-filled room, my projector whirs, and "Pocono Fly Fishing with the Reverend Sam Huffard" flashes on the screen. Then comes artist Ned Smith's scratch-board impressionistic illustrations of a trout's view of a Black Nose Dace minnow besides its bucktail counterpart in a stiff current. Standing by the screen with a pointer, I call attention to the striking resemblance and explain the theory behind streamer fishing. Then the screen fills with a vividly colored, sylvan tableau, in the center of which the six-foot-two Reverend Sam stands shin deep in a glistening riffle quartering a streamer against its flow.

As Sam Huffard casts and retrieves, I discuss the function of the fly rod and line versus that of spinning and bait-casting tackle. The rod describes a pulsating arch as Sam's streamer is grabbed by a small trout. He nets the fish sloppily (on purpose) against the current. The next fish—a handsome 10-inch brookie—is permitted to run. After careful playing, this trout is properly netted, with the current's help, and I discuss the whys and wherefores of playing and landing.

While Sam moves smoothly downstream, I note the finer points of his tactics: the jerking action he gives his rod tip in order to impart a darting, minnowlike action to the streamer; the hand-twist retrieve; and the targeting of his streamer through false casts.

Now the scene gives way to the next section, "The Wet Fly-Nymph." Impressionistic drawings show a natural fly hatching and an artificial wet fly, both just below the surface. I explain the phenomena of hatching aquatic flies and how trout feed on them. Sam demonstrates the need for upstream presentation of the corresponding counterfeits on another Pocono stream. A typical, slow nymph-take follows. Sam sets the hook smartly and plays a lovely 14-inch brown trout.

The final section, "The Dry Fly," shows a surface-borne natural fly next to an artificial imitation. I elucidate. Sam presents a dry fly, which is shown floating, close up, and is then taken by a 10-inch brownie. High-jumping acrobatics follow, accompanied by muffled exclamations from the audience. When the movie ends and the lights are turned up, a hundred sportsmen applaud more than politely and prove I've had them *with* me during the show.

Sam Huffard came to my church in Gap, Pennsylvania, from seminary, with a desire to master fly fishing, I tell the sportsmen. A sometime worm-dunker, he was overawed at the prospect of joining me on a Pocono trip, but after taking his first trout on a fly Sam was hooked. After two more trips he developed sufficient confidence to preclude any future reversion to worms. We made occasional trips over 10 years; then, I explain, when Sam felt that his mission in Gap was comp-

132

leted, he accepted a call from the First Presbyterian Church of East Stroudsburg, Pennsylvania, in the heart of the Poconos. He now fishes more than his onetime mentor!

Questions and answers and refreshments follow. Then I disassemble my gear, set off on icy roads, and arrive home at midnight.

The event described above is typical of many I experienced during winter evenings in 1969 and 1970. I made the film with the most basic of "home movie" cameras. I worked without a tripod, filters, and experience, so results were amateurish. But after my company's advertising agency reproduced those descriptive headers from Ned Smith's art *(Simplified Fly Fishing)* I felt that the film served its purpose: the explanation of fly-fishing theory and practice in simple terms.

When I first showed it to a service club I was pleased with the reception. One of Lancaster County's many sportsmen's clubs soon contacted me: Would I show the movie and give my talk?

The Pennsylvania Federation of Sportsmen Clubs has thousands of members comprising hundreds of clubs spread across the Commonwealth. There are four in a radius of eight miles from my home. These clubs do a superb job in game conservation. They fight hard and with some success for clean waters. But they represent the most powerful force in the state behind "put and take" concepts in trout fishing. The vast majority of their members equate successful trout management with optimum hatchery production. At best, fly anglers are generally looked upon as snobs; at worst, enemies, bent upon commandeering prime open water for themselves in the name of "flies only."

Lost on them is the fact that waters regulated for "flies only" and "catch and release" make for more effective trout conservation; hence, more trout for all. The biggest factor perpetuating the anti-fly bias is the myth that fly fishing is for experts only, a belief often promulgated by fly anglers themselves in order to keep their pastime in the realm of the esoteric. I wrote my book to help to dispel the erroneous idea that fly fishing is difficult to master. Unlike the book's shotgun effect, the film's approach is riflelike, directed at those who can—if only on a regional level—directly influence trout management policies: the sportsmen's clubs.

The great majority of Pennsylvania sportsmen's clubs are located near trout waters—or, more properly, waters that are regularly stocked with trout. Generally, members help to stock, often on land they themselves own. But the clubs frown on the state-imposed flies-only regulation of such waters. The Pennsylvania Fish Commission is willing to expand fly regulated water—when landowners and interested parties approve. But when a project is embarked upon, there is no assurance that it will be permanent, for said interested parties must remain sold.

Sam Hall, the local waterway patrolman, began to interest a sportsmen's club on the Octorara Creek in southern Lancaster County in the Donegal story. Even though fly fishermen in this club were as scarce as hen's teeth, an improvement project for flies-only was soon under way. Stream beautification and public recognition for it provided incentives. Our T.U. group spent a day working with the sportsmen in the stream, then held a cookout in the evening. Camaraderie reigned. Friendships were born. I was asked to show my film, and our T.U. chapter arranged to recognize the club's efforts by awarding a plaque. Sam Hall, the prime mover, also received a plaque, and the ceremony was well covered in the press.

Since my film and spiel came after these events, I could be accused of "backing modestly into the limelight," to parody the late Westbrook Pegler. This was not the case, for it isn't always convenient to brave winter-bound roads at night in search of these off-the-beaten-path clubhouses. Rather, my effort was directed toward maintaining membership interest, hopefully by converting spin and bait fishermen through demonstrating, graphically, that fly fishing can be easy to learn.

I soon developed a technique in dealing with the club audiences who see the film. From the mass of string-tie-festooned lumber shirts, I try to distinguish two groups: older and sometimes bored-looking members, and the youngest, usually the most avid listeners. During the refreshment period I socialize with both groups. I've marked the first for confirmed bait fishermen, more often than not meat fishermen. In quiet asides I tell them that fly-fishing-only stretches are more heavily stocked with larger fish—that bait fishing "below the wire" is terrific, particularly after high water abets the downstream movement of fish. When their faces light up I know that baser instincts have been appeased, and they will not oppose a fly-regulated project.

Young people, not being inured to one form of fishing, are usually open to new approaches. And only a few youthful fly fishermen in such groups can carry a lot of weight, for it takes a pretty mean "sportsman" to rob kids of chances to improve their fishing skills and pleasure. Not to mention that the conservation angle weighs heavily with youngsters, thanks to the new, ecology-oriented school curricula. So I always concentrate heavily on the most receptive of the young people present.

I first recognized the importance of youth in advancing the cause of fly angling during the 1968 annual campfire and outing of the Brotherhood of the Jungle Cock, a worthwhile conservation organization founded by the late, great Joe Brooks and some friends 30 years ago to popularize fly fishing among youth. I attended my first meeting with my godson, Chester Gibson, who knew little about fly fishing when we arrived at the campsite in Thurmont, Maryland. But after a weekend of stream and pond fly casting, fly tying and lectures, he became a true believer. I was asked to bring my movie, but when I discovered that my friend Joe Brooks would be there, I hid the projector and tried to duck this part of the program. I could not bring myself to show the film in the presence of one who has had a hand in making superb outdoor film productions. Joe insisted, and I finally relented. He later said that the film suited our program perfectly, and he praised the idea behind it.

Boy Scout troops and boys clubs are now on my lecture circuit, along with merchant and business groups. Lancaster's Pennsylvania Dutch country has now become one of the nation's top tourist attractions, and the availability of fly-fishing water for discriminating out-of-state sportsmen can provide additional strings for the bows of alert promoters of tourism.

Fly anglers have a tremendous and never-ending fight to wage on the ecology front. But we must remember that quality fly angling cannot be advanced if better trout management practices do not progress concurrently. So it is my considered opinion that we must sell our pastime to those who, paradoxically, can do the most to advance its cause—the non-fly fisherman.

Angling authors often wind up their books with clarion calls for rededication to the cause of clean, free-flowing streams and a pollutant-free environment. Some of these paeans to the great outdoors are in a Smokey the Bear vein: invocations against littering, fish killing, and so on. Others are more specific, in decrying dam building and industrial pollution. All such blurbs have two things in common. They are aimed at the already converted and they champion endeavors which individuals—as individuals—can do little to advance. This is not to suggest that fly anglers can't help to solve problems affecting their own watersheds. Work of this sort is progressing spectacularly across the country, a prime example being the "water watching" program pioneered by the Theodore Gordon Fly Fishers in New York State. But the big conflicts involving the federal bulldozer require group efforts on behalf of all varieties of increasing numbers of conservationists.

Individual fly tyers can do more to create instant conservationists faster and in greater quantities (through conducting fly-tying classes) than all the sermonizing scribes put together. There are, of course, many fishermen who don't tie or even fish flies who work mightily for clean waters. But my own experience generally bears out Charlie Fox's contention that fly tyers "become more dedicated anglers, and it's the dedicated anglers who are today carrying the fight for proper trout management."

George Harvey and I hope that our book will help fledgling fly tyers discover fly fishing's "other dimension." We hope, too, that experienced tying anglers will find new and useful information that will lead to more enjoyable hours with their vises and long rods.

INDEX

Numbers in *italic* denote illustrations

Turkey-wing quill, 52, *52*
Tying thread, 22, *25*, 49, *49*

Van Gytenbeck, Pete, 41

Wet flies, 42–45
  hook sizes for, 21
  suggested patterns, 61
  tail materials for, 23

tying, 54–60
upstream presentation of, 42–44
White Maribu streamer, 12, 13–14, 27
Wing materials, 23
Winged ant imitations, 97–98, 105
Wise, Jack, III, 8
Wise, John S., Jr., 115
Wool bodies, 53, 61, 90